PROVINCIAL FRENCH COOKING

PROVINCIAL FRENCH COOKING

HELGE RUBINSTEIN

HEARST BOOKS

NEW YORK

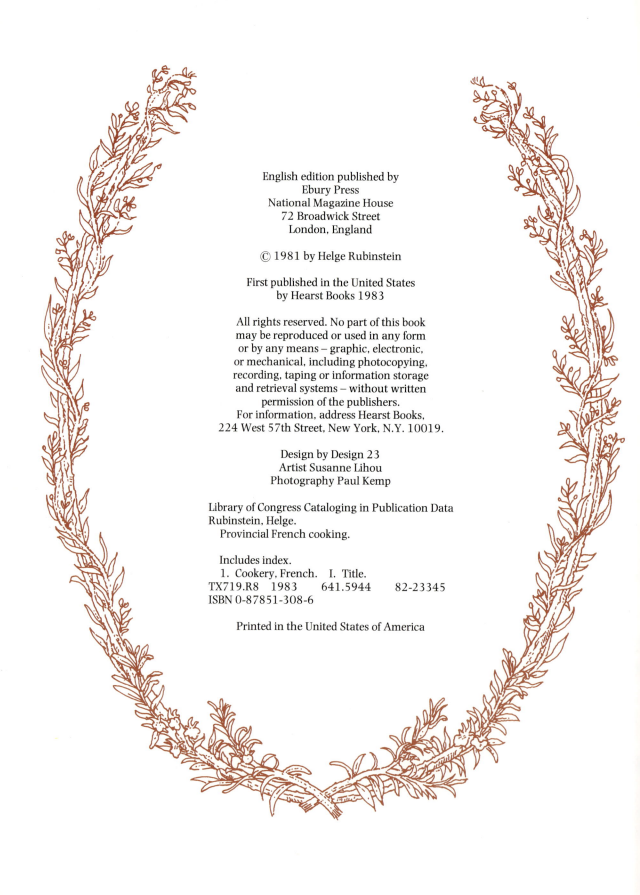

English edition published by
Ebury Press
National Magazine House
72 Broadwick Street
London, England

© 1981 by Helge Rubinstein

First published in the United States
by Hearst Books 1983

Design by Design 23
Artist Susanne Lihou
Photography Paul Kemp

Library of Congress Cataloging in Publication Data
Rubinstein, Helge.
  Provincial French cooking.

  Includes index.
  1. Cookery, French.   I. Title.
TX719.R8   1983   641.5944   82-23345
ISBN 0-87851-308-6

Printed in the United States of America

Contents

Introduction

A journey through France is a feast for all the senses. It is a country of great variety and contrast, rich in history. In France every region has its own specialties – in food as much as in landscape and architecture.

A land the size of France, with three distinct coastlines, two mountain ranges – the Alps and the Pyrenees – at opposite corners, as well as the Massif Central in the middle, has a wide range of climatic conditions. Wherever you go, therefore, the local produce has its own special characteristics, and so has the cuisine, for the French cook, be it housewife or chef, has a fine respect for raw materials, and the cooking will be designed to make the best of what is available locally.

In *Provincial French Cooking*, we have divided our exploration into two parts. The introduction takes us on a tour through the bounty of France, from the flat, northeast corner of Flanders, through the rocky coastline of Western Brittany, to the salt-marshes of the Carmargue in the South. These pages constitute a roving appreciation of the meat and game, vegetables, fruit and cheeses of the world's most favored cuisine. They are followed by pages of recipes which enable armchair travelers to bring the richness of France into their kitchens. Each recipe – whether appetizer, main course, side dish or dessert – has the region of its origin noted below the name. And given some careful saving, preliminary planning and a good deal of anticipation, there is nothing to stop the peripatetic reader from taking this wide but specialized knowledge of French regional cooking as the basis for gastronomic forays into the mother country itself.

We begin in Brittany, with its megalithic stones and roadside calvaries, and above all, its varied coastline. At times rocky and perilous, at others flat and marshy, it provides an abundance of seafood and shellfish. On to neighboring Normandy, country of lush pastures and rich dairy products, as well as home of William the Conqueror and the Bayeax tapestry. The soaring Gothic cathedrals are the pride of the north-eastern part of France, which bears the rather heavier Flemish and German influences in its cooking, with solid, warming pork and onion-based dishes, graced by the flinty wines of Alsace. Between the two lies the Île de France, with Paris, capital city of *haute cuisine* and home of great restaurants since the time of the Revolution, at its center.

As we move further south, we come to the country of the Loire and its tributaries, with lovely chateaux reflected in the rivers. Here freshwater fish and light Loire wines predominate, while a little further down in Burgundy, in the very heart of France, we can enjoy the fine Charollais beef, the plump yellow chickens of Bresse and the great Burgundy wines. Approaching the center of France we come to the area of the Dordogne and the great gorges of the Tarn, to the country where Romanesque churches and romantic landscapes delight the eye, and the rich pâtés and truffles of the Perigord are feasts for the palate.

Here we begin to meet the two chief flavors of the South, garlic and olive oil, and the further south we go, the more these two flavors dominate, coupled with the profusion of fruit and vegetables from Provence, country of Van Gogh landscapes, rich in remains from its Roman past. When we finally reach the southern coast, there is the many-splendored seafood of the Mediterranean. Going westwards towards the Atlantic coast and along the Pyrenees, we find the Basque and Spanish influence in the cuisine, while the towns and fortresses resonate with echoes from the Middle Ages, and Roland's Roncevalles is still the pass into Spain.

No wonder that with so much local history, France is still a country of well-defined provinces. I have used their old historic names rather than the modern *département* equivalents, for these are the borders that still count from the gastronomic point of view. Even with modern methods of refrigeration and fast transport, and the growth of convenience, especially frozen, foods, which the French housewife is far too canny to despise, French cooking has retained its regional character. In spite of the fact that one of the earliest known cook books was written by a Frenchman, the great Taillevent, master-cook to Charles VI, cook books are used much less here than in other countries, and traditions are still handed down from mother to daughter – and from father to son.

For all its strong roots, French cooking is still breaking new ground. But although the "nouvelle cuisine" has no place in this book, which is about the traditional cooking of provincial France, it too follows the fundamental tenet of good cooking, which is a basic respect – or love – for the raw materials. *Faites simples* is the laconic ground-rule given by Escoffier, author of the classic *Guide Culinaire*, and he stands well rooted in the tradition of his forebears. We have only to look at the *Trés Riches Heures du Duc de Berry* to see how lovingly the 15th-century artists portrayed the pleasures of the table. Happily, the French have no puritan tradition, and their love of food remains unrepentant.

The traveler through France – both footloose tourist and our reader – has the opportunity to share these pleasures. *Bon voyage et bon appetit.*

Brittany, Maine and Touraine

The 2,175 mile long crenelated coastline of Brittany dominates the life of the region, and the rich variety of seafood is its chief gastronomic glory. This is not an area for elaborate dishes or extravagant sauces; indeed, until the last century, Brittany was quite poor, so there is no tradition of a sophisticated cuisine.

But nothing can rival the abundance of shellfish caught all around its coast: the lobsters from the rocky promontories of the most westerly tip of France, the crabs, spider crabs, scallops, clams, langoustines and shrimp, and above all the oysters, the Belon oyster the most famous among them, reared in the oyster beds of the gulf of Morbihan. Brittany was one of the first areas to go in for oyster cultivation, and is still one of the few places where even the most dedicated oyster lover may be heard to say "Oh, no, not oysters again!" Even more plentiful and less expensive than oysters are the little shiny blue-black mussels that cluster on thick posts or *buchots* set into the shallow marshy sea bed along the southwest coast, and which are harvested in special flat-bottomed boats at low tide, a method that is said to have been discovered here (by accident, like all the best inventions) by a ship-wrecked Irishman in the thirteenth century. It has changed little since. Shellfish, along with mackerel, monkfish, sole, cod and above all sardines, make the fish markets and stalls one of the most exciting places to visit in the coastal Breton towns.

Then there are the famous *pré-salé* lambs, the lambs reared in the tide-washed salty meadows around Mont St Michel, tender and tasty, and the gray sea-salt itself that is panned in that area, and which, dirty and unpromising though it may look, gives the cooking of the region some of its special flavor.

Inland Brittany also has its market gardens, and Roscoff is famous for its firm, long-lasting onions, and still sends out a fleet of bicycling onion sellers every year; Nantes prides itself on its carrots; the artichokes of St Brieuc are fat and full to bursting, and the strawberries of Plougastel are highly prized for their flavor. There are special greengages which grow in this northern part of France which owe their name to Claude of Brittany, Queen to Francois I.

Brittany's national dish is the crêpe, the huge buckwheat pancake which can be bought from stalls at street corners, or eaten at *crêperies*, specialized small restaurants where you can make a whole meal of crêpes, starting with savory fillings, and ending with a final *crêpe au chocolat* – accompanied by the local cider.

As you move further east into Maine and Touraine, a land of kings and poets, the landscape becomes gentler and the cooking more refined. The river Loire is full of salmon, pike (most honored in the restaurant dish, *quenelles de brochet*), shad and trout, to be served with the delicate *beurre blanc*.

This is a land of orchards and pig farms, with such farmhouse conserves as *rillettes de porc* in every charcuterie window, and fresh cheeses, such as the *cremets* of Angers, a cream cheese to be eaten with sugar and cream, and goat's cheeses, such as the famous St Maure, to be found in the markets.

A gentle cuisine, to be accompanied by the delicate, fresh Loire wines.

Normandy

Sunbaked and contented, that is how Normandy strikes the summer traveler, with its prosperous farmsteads and fertile orchards – and no hint of the fighting that has time and again swept across these fields from the Vikings onwards, right up to 1944.

Nature has been generous to Normandy. Its coastline is long and produces an enviable variety of seafood: not only the sole for which Normandy is famous, but also lobsters and langoustines, shrimp and scallops, oysters and mussels, turbot, mackerel and herring. The coast is washed by the Gulf Stream, so that the climate is temperate.

The lush pastures are grazed by sleek and placid cows, whose products are the pride of Normandy. A visit to a dairy shop is a joy. Here, in spotlessly clean, probably tiled surroundings, you will see great mounds of the freshest butter – the best is said to come from Issigny, on the north coast – deep yellow if it is slightly salted, paler if unsalted, from which you may cut a block as large or small as you wish. Stoneware jars, blue-patterned outside, gray inside, hold quantities of *crème fraîche*, the thick, slightly acidulated cream that is such a prominent feature of Norman

cooking, to be ladled out and sold by weight. Here too you can buy fresh cream cheeses, such as *fromage blanc, petits suisses* and others. And, as you drive through the smaller towns and villages of Normandy, you realize that every other place sounds like a cheese – Camembert, Livarot, Pont-L'Evêque, La Bouille, Neufchâtel.

Everywhere there are apple orchards. Best of all are said to be the apples from the Vallée d'Auge, from which the many meat dishes which use apples get their name. Cider, sweet or dry, sparkling or still, is one of the chief products of the area, and every farm in the region seems to advertise its own homemade variety. In restaurants it is served throughout the meal, up to and including the dessert, which in any case is often the famous *tarte normande*.

Calvados is the eau-de-vie made from apples, and it too is often distilled and sold by individual proprietors. It is matured in casks for up to ten years, and is drunk after meals or as a *trou normand*, a digestif drunk in the middle of the meal to make room for the next course.

Benedictine, the liqueur distilled from a variety of herbs, is also a native of Normandy, and is still made near Fécamp where it was first brewed by a sixteenth century monk.

Rouen is the gastronomic capital of Normandy, and when you have marveled at its beautiful cathedral, it is time to feast your eyes on the food stores, notably the pâtisseries which glint and sparkle like jewelers, and the charcuteries, as amusing and as colorful as toy stores. Rouen is especially famous for its ducks, which have an almost gamey flavor. From them pâtés and galantines are made, all temptingly displayed in the charcuterie windows, together with many different kinds of sausages, especially black puddings, or *boudins*, and the famous *tripe à la mode de Caen*.

When you have spent a little time in Normandy you will no longer be surprised at Mme Bovary's wedding feast, held at Pont-Audemer, where they sat down "forty-three to a table and remained there sixteen hours".

Alsace, Lorraine and Franche-Comté

We are so used to thinking of Alsace and Lorraine in one breath, that we forget that they are really quite separate regions, with very different histories.

Lorraine was an independent dukedom until midway through the eighteenth century when Louis XV acquired it and made his father-in-law, Stanislas Leszczynski, the deposed king of Poland, governor and Duke of Lorraine. Not only does Nancy owe Stanislas the grace and elegance of its central square, which is named after him, but Stanislas also seems to have been responsible for many happy inventions in food. It was he who first soaked plain cakes in sweet wine or rum, and so invented the rum baba; his cook, Madeleine, is said to have been the first to make the little fluted cakes that bear her name, and it was one of his pâtissiers who thought of filling puff pastry cases with a mixture of chicken and mushrooms in cream sauce. They were sent to Marie, Stanislas' daughter, and have been known as *bouchées à la reine* ever since.

Cakes, pastry, preserves and confectionery still play a large part in the cooking of the area. There are the quiches, perhaps the best-known of the specialties of Lorraine, and also macaroons, gingerbreads and airy little doughnuts wickedly known as *pets de nonne*. Bar-le-Duc, the old seat of the dukes of Lorraine, specializes in beautiful, jewel-like fruit preserves; Metz has its *fraises de*

Metz, crystalized strawberries, and Nancy its *bergamots de Nancy*, the bergamot-flavored little hard candies.

Alsace, which shares the Rhine as a border with Germany, has had many years of German domination, and the influence of Germany is very marked in the food, especially in the prominence of pork. *Choucroûte garni* is probably the best known Alsatian specialty, and a formidable dish it is, with its mountain of sauerkraut topped with smoked pork, smoked ham and the numerous different pork sausages of the region. Goose is the other great specialty, and the *pâté de foie gras* of Strasbourg is almost as famous as its cathedral.

Alsace is of course primarily a wine-growing area, and a trip through the wine villages, especially at the time of the grape harvest, is like a visit to a highly modernized Ruritania, with immaculately kept (sometimes rebuilt) medieval villages. The cooking here, as so often in wine-growing areas, is of the very finest, and the area around Illhaeusern is as thickly studded with Michelin stars as any in France. To end an Alsatian meal there will be an eau-de-vie, distilled from one of the many soft or stone fruit that grow so richly here. Kirsch is the best known, but *framboise* and *myrtilles* also have a miraculous bouquet.

The Franche-Comté, further south, is a beautiful area of peaks, forests and streams familiar from the paintings of Courbet, whose homeland it was. There are fresh trout from mountain streams; crayfish, which are the basis of the coral pink *sauce Nantua*; good mountain food such as smoked sausages with picturesque names like *Jésus* and *gendarmes*, and good hard cheeses, especially the Comté cheese which is excellent for cooking and eating alike. Perhaps the greatest pleasure of all are the many different mushrooms that can be found in the woods.

Ile de France, Paris and Orléanais

The Ile de France, with Paris at its center, is and has been for centuries the very heart of France. It is not an area that has developed very specific characteristics of its own, but Paris is traditionally the center of all excellence, the birth place of haute cuisine as well as of haute couture.

Since the time of the Revolution, when grand households were dissolved and some of the chefs from the nobility started the first restaurants, Paris has been the home of some of the world's most renowned *tables*, devoted to cooking as one of the fine arts. For this, it is singularly well placed, for all the best ingredients from all over the country have always been brought to the capital and have

Glossary

Bake blind To bake flan, tart and tartlet pastry shells without a filling. The pastry may be lined with cooking parchment paper and dried beans or foil, or small tartlet cases may just be pricked with a fork.

Baste To moisten meat, poultry or game during roasting by spooning over it the juices and melted fat from the pan. This prevents the food from drying out, adds extra flavor and improves the appearance.

Beurre manié A liaison of butter and flour kneaded together to a paste. Used for thickening soups or stews after cooking is complete. Whisk a little of the paste into the hot liquid and bring back to a boil, adding a little more until the required thickness is reached.

Blanch To treat food with boiling water in order to whiten it; to preserve its natural color; to loosen its skin; to remove any strong or bitter taste; to kill unwanted enzymes before freezing or preserving.

Bouquet garni A small bunch of herbs tied together in cheesecloth and used to give flavor to stews and casseroles. A simple bouquet garni consists of a sprig each of parsley and thyme, a bay leaf, 2 cloves and a few peppercorns.

Canapés Appetizers, consisting as a rule of slices of bread cut into various sizes – usually quite small – used plain or fried, topped with savory tidbits.

Core To remove the hard, indigestible center of certain foods, particularly fruits such as apples, pears and pineapples. The term is also used to describe removing the center of kidneys.

Croûte 1 A large round or finger of toasted bread, about ¼ inch thick, on which game and some entrées and savories are served.

Croûte 2 A pastry crust.

Croûtons Small pieces of bread which are fried or toasted and served as an accompaniment to soup or salad or as a garnish.

Crème fraîche This is cream, found widely in France which has matured and fermented to the point where it has thickened slightly and has a faintly acid taste. To make a similar substitute see page 118.

Crush To break down food into smaller particles either, as in the case of spices in a pestle and mortar, or garlic through a garlic press, to release the flavor in cooking or to make a crumb-like texture, as with cookies, for mixing with other ingredients.

Cut up To divide poultry, game birds or small animals such as rabbits into suitable portions for cooking.

En croûte Encrusted, wrapped or enclosed in pastry before cooking.

Flambé Used to describe a dish flavored with flamed alcohol. Alcohol (usually brandy or sherry) is ignited and allowed to burn either on the finished dish or in the pan during cooking.

Glaze To give a glossy surface to sweet or savory dishes before or after cooking. Various substances are used for different foods. The glaze improves both appearance and flavor.

flowed through its markets and shops. Moreover, the surrounding countryside of the Ile de France with its mild and even climate, is like a gigantic market garden, and almost every small district in the area has its own specialty to offer, be it a raw material or a special dish.

Some of the best potatoes and beans are grown in the area around Soissons; Crécy is so famous for its carrots that any dish with its name is enough to signify that carrots are among the ingredients. The area around Orléans, in the Loire valley, also produces some of the best green and root vegetables, and has become one of the centers of the canning industry of France. The forests around Paris and Fontainebleau have always provided plentiful game and a great variety of mushrooms, while *champignons de Paris*, the little white button mushrooms, have been cultivated in caves and disused quarries around Paris for centuries. Paris itself was once surrounded by orchards, and some of its suburbs are still full of fruit trees, especially Montmorency, well known for its fat, tart cherries.

To the south of Paris are the wheatfields of the Beauce area. You can see the great cathedral of Chartres floating in the distance above the plain as you drive towards the city. This ready supply of wheat has helped to make Paris the home of some of the best bread in the world. The Parisian *baguette*, and all its many fatter and thinner cousins, eaten within a few hours of baking with fresh Normandy butter, is quite simply one of the most delectable pleasures in life. And then there is the whole complex art of the pastry cook, nowhere more highly developed than in Paris, where every pâtissier is a craftsman, making not only his own croissants and brioches, but also éclairs, mille-feuilles, gâteaux and petits-fours.

The area has many other specialties. There is the special granular mustard in its white earthenware pot called Meaux, that derives its name from the city just northwest of Paris. There are the wild strawberries of Rambouillet; the famous cheeses from Coulommiers and from Brie – the latter dubbed "the king of cheeses" by Talleyrand; the honey from the Gatinais area; and some of the world's best vinegar from Orléans, for it is here that vinegar was first made from wine that would not travel. From Fontainebleau come the fine Chasselas grapes, reputedly among the first to be cultivated for the table. And the town of Chantilly has given its name to the delicate light whipped cream of French pâtisseries.

No wonder that, with such surroundings, Paris has long been the gastronomic capital of Europe, mecca for all worshippers of the table.

Knead To work a dough firmly, using the knuckles for bread-making, the fingertips in pastry-making. In both cases the outside of the dough is drawn into the center.

Langues de chats Literally cats' tongues; small, thin, flat, crisp cookies.

Lard To insert small strips of fat bacon into the flesh of game birds, poultry and meat before cooking to prevent it drying out when roasting. A special larding needle is used. Today, because of the quality of our meat, it is usually used more for decorative effect.

Line To give a protective or decorative covering to the bottom and sides of a cooking container – eg. with cooking parchment paper when baking cakes; with pastry when making tarts; or with bacon for pâtés.

Marinate To steep raw meat, game or fish in a blend of oil, wine or vinegar and seasonings for periods of an hour up to several days to make it more tender and flavorsome, and to give moisture to dry meats.

Mouli-légumes An inexpensive food mill found in most French kitchens, used for puréeing foods.

Pâte Pastry, especially pâte sucrée, a sweet flan pastry.

Poach To cook gently in a liquid at simmering point so that the surface is just trembling. It can be done in an open pan, in the oven or using an egg poacher with a lid. The term is used most commonly for eggs and fish.

Punch down To knead dough for a second time on a lightly floured surface for 2–3 minutes after rising. This removes large bubbles and ensures an even texture.

Purée To sieve, blend or pound raw or cooked foods so that they are of a creamy, lump-free texture. If using a sieve, a wire one may be used for meat and vegetables but a nylon one is best for fruit and tomatoes.

Press To shape meat by pressing it under a weight. The cold pressed meat – often spiced meat or tongue, boned stuffed chicken or meat roll – is turned out and sometimes glazed. Some fruit desserts are also pressed.

Reduce To fast boil a liquid (especially when making a soup, sauce or syrup) in an uncovered pan, in order to evaporate surplus liquid and concentrate flavor.

Rise To allow a yeast dough to double in size before baking. When it has risen, the dough is sometimes punched down, shaped and then allowed to rise for a second time.

Scald To pour boiling water over fruit (eg. tomatoes, peaches) to make it easy to remove skins. Remove food before it cooks. Also to treat milk or to cleanse jelly bags.

Skim To take off the surface of stock, gravy, stews, etc. or scum from other foods (eg. jams) while they are cooking. A piece of paper towel or a metal spoon may be used.

Terrine China or earthenware dish used for pâtés and potted meats, also general term for food cooked in a terrine.

Truffle A rare fungus of the same family as the mushroom. Either black or white (rarely red).

Truss To tie or skewer a bird into a compact shape before cooking.

Charentes, Poitou and Limousin

The flat, silted coastline of the Charentes Maritime is a continuation of the southern coast of Brittany, and it shares much the same rich haul of Atlantic seafood as its northern neighbor – from tuna, swordfish and even sturgeon, down to sardines and tiny elvers. The specialty of La Rochelle, the big Atlantic seaport, is the *chaudrée*, from the archaic French word for cauldron – a great stew or soup made from all the fish, large and small, that come into the port. Oysters and mussels are farmed here too, and the creamy *mouclade* is as popular here as in southern Brittany, while the Ile d'Oleron, just off the coast, has the biggest shrimp fishing industry in France.

The marshy pastures just inland feed cattle and sheep, and produce *pré-salé* lamb as tender and as well flavored as the lambs of Brittany. Further inland, large snails, called *cagouilles* grow fat in the vineyards, and "*cagouillard*" is a favorite insult to throw at the local inhabitants, accusing them of snail-like sluggishness.

The most famous product of the area is cognac, the world-renowned pure brandy made from the wine of a strictly defined area, and matured in casks of oak from neighboring Limousin. Visitors should certainly go to see the vaults of at least one of the great brandy houses in the town of Cognac itself, belonging to Martell, Hennessy, Otard and such great names as these.

Market gardening is a flourishing local industry, producing, in particular, the famous, fragrant Charentais melons, and this is the beginning of the garlic growing and eating south.

In Poitou, in the northern part of this region, and in the Limousin, we enter a fertile area of rich farmland and market gardens, where beans, zucchini, artichokes, cauliflowers and, above all, cabbages are grown. This is an area of rich and comfortable food, with hams from the Vendée, conserves of duck and goose, game and mushrooms from the forests (the famous dish *lièvre à la royale*, which takes all day to prepare, comes from Limoges) and goat cheeses, especially the creamy Chabichou and the Pyramide from Poitou.

Above all, the area is rich in chestnuts and walnuts. Chestnut trees line the roads, to be gathered by the fistful by passers-by. They are used in every kind of dish, both sweet and savory. There is the *purée limousine*, a purée of cabbage or sprouts and chestnuts; they are served braised as a vegetable to be eaten on its own; they are made into a flour for bread and cakes, and they are also candied to make *marrons glacés*, to export around the world. The local walnut oil, once used by painters to mix their delicate colors, is much prized. It must be used very fresh, and has a unique flavor, every bit as rich, and with a special pungency of its own, as the olive oil from further south.

Artois, Flanders, Picardy and Champagne

Artois, Flanders and Picardy are low-lying areas like their neighbor, Belgium, and the temperament of the country, as of its people, is sturdy and steady, in spite of the many scenes of fighting that have taken place over the centuries on its land and beaches.

Herring and mackerel are caught off the coast, especially around Dunkirk and Calais, and they are eaten, smoked and salted as well as fresh, in *matelotes*, or fish stews. Further along the coast, at Wimereux near Boulogne, once an elegant seaside resort, the local people pride themselves on cultivating some of the best mussels – small, dark blue, and with an excellent flavor. In the bay of Le Crotoy you can eat wonderful hors d'oeuvre of small shellfish, or jellied eels or a fish soup known in these parts as a *chaudière*.

Wild boar is still hunted in the densely wooded area of the Ardennes, and pork features prominently in the region's robust country cooking. Ardennes ham, smoked to a deep red color, is a specialty, and pork sausages, *boudins* or blood sausages, including a special *boudin blanc*, and *andouillettes*, or tripe sausages, are eaten alone or in such hearty dishes as the *hochepot*, hefty northern cousin to the *pot au feu*. Such meals are usually accompanied by beer, for this is one of the few areas of France where no wine is produced locally.

There is other game too, and *pâté de bécasse* (woodcock pâté) and duck pie, or *canard en croûte*, are specialties of Amiens.

Vegetables are mostly root vegetables or cabbage, often cooked with the meat or made into a pie, such as the Flemish specialty, the creamy *flamiche de poireaux*.

Desserts in this area are substantial too, and tend to be tarts, fritters or puddings. But the town of Cambrai, whose fortune is based on the wool and cloth trade, has a charming specialty of delicate little mint-flavored pillow-shaped sweets, known as *bêtises de Cambrai*, for they are said to have been a *bêtise* or mistake made by an apprentice.

The countryside of Champagne, as its name (derived from the word for field) implies, is flat, or gently hilly with wide vistas of plains, and the rivers and streams that run across it provide carp, pike and trout. The town of Rheims, with its great and historic cathedral in which the kings of France were crowned, has its specialty, a ham in pastry case, as well as a special pear called *rousselet*, which is traditionally offered to visiting monarchs or heads of state, but is too juicy to travel. The real glory of the area lies in its world famous wine, which, to be truly champagne, must be made from grapes grown in a strictly defined area. The process of making champagne was developed by a seventeenth century Benedictine monk, Dom Perignon, who was born in St. Ménéhould, now more associated with its specialty, broiled pig's feet. The process of making champagne, which has been refined and perfected since Dom Perignon discovered a way of preserving the sparkling quality of the wine, is a long and fascinating one, and travelers in this area should visit at least one of the famous champagne houses and its *caves*.

Burgundy, Nivernais, Berry and Bourbonnais

For lovers of good food and good wine, Burgundy is a paradise on earth. Few other regions in France are so richly endowed with the products of nature, and in none has human skill embellished them so deliciously as here.

The great white Charollais cattle originate from this area and are still most at home in the lush pastureland of the Charolles area, though they are now exported to other parts of France. They produce the tenderest, leanest and best flavored of beef. The pigs from the wilder parts of the region provide the tangy smoked Morvan hams. And then there are the plump, tasty chickens from Bresse, the only chickens that have an *appellatiôn controlée*, like a fine wine.

The Burgundian snails are the fattest of all, and the charcuterie shops are full of their pretty shells already plugged with garlic butter. The woods are full of game: venison, pheasant and woodcock, hare and wild rabbit. The rivers and streams offer ample crayfish, pike and trout.

Vegetables grow well in this fertile area, notably onions and carrots. *Nivernaise*, describing a dish, is enough to indicate that it is garnished with glazed carrots and onions, while *bourguignonne* usually indicates that diced bacon or smoked ham is also used with the carrots and onions, as well as red Burgundian wine. Mushrooms, and even truffles, are to be found, and fruit, especially pears and cherries, ripen in profusion.

Add to such natural endowment the skills developed over centuries, (you have only to look at the *Très Riches Heures* of the Duc de Berry to see the love of good things), and you have a cuisine that is rich and varied, but never over-elaborate. The great Burgundian dishes are not sophisticated restaurant productions. But such classics as *pouchouse*, the stew of freshwater fish, *boeuf bourguignonne*, *lapin à la moutarde*, *carottes Vichy* and *gougère*, are all dishes that belong to an area that has enjoyed centuries of prosperity and that has refined its cooking without ever losing the country origins of its cuisine.

There are also specialties associated with particular towns or districts. Dijon is of course world-famous for its mustards made with verjus, the juice of unripened grapes, but it also prides itself on its spiced honey cakes (*pain d'épices*) and the famous *jambon persillé*.

Wine is really the most important product of the area, and each region produces its own distinctive wine, which is the foundation of its wealth. No stay in Burgundy, however brief, is complete without at least a visit to the beautiful fifteenth-century Hotel Dieu at Beaune, still the site for one of the most important wine auctions of the year. Apart from wine, Burgundy also produces two marvelous drinks; first, *marc de bourgogne*, distilled from the residue of grapes after the pressing, a powerful but full-flavored eau-de-vie, excellent for flavoring meat dishes or fruit salads, unless it is so mature that this would be sacrilege; and, secondly, *cassis*, one of the great specialties of the region, a liqueur distilled from black currants, and invaluable for flavoring fruit desserts and ices, as well as making, with the addition of chilled white wine, the excellent and increasingly popular aperitif, *kir*.

Guyenne, Gascogne and Béarn

One of the most historic corners of France – it was here, in the Dordogne area of Guyenne, that Cro-Magnon man was found, and the prehistoric cave-paintings of Les Eyzies still astonish the visitor with their freshness and vigor – this is also an area of fine wines, rich food and pungent flavors.

There are delicious specialties all over the region. The long, straight Atlantic coastline provides tuna, squid and sardines, while oysters are farmed in the bay of Arcachon and are often eaten here, Spanish style, with spicy little sausages. The Basque influence is strong in this south-western corner of France, with tomatoes and peppers, especially the *piment basque* (almost, but not quite, as fiery as a chili pepper) providing a dominant taste. The salt-cured hams of Bayonne, whose quality is still watched over by a "brotherhood", have a strong individual character and are exported all over the world. This is also

one of the first parts of France to be introduced to chocolate, brought by the Jews from Spain and Portugal in the sixteenth century, and it is still a chocolate-manufacturing area. The Béarn is the birthplace of Henri IV, the king whose pious wish it was that all his subjects should have a chicken in their pot on Sundays, and the *poule au pot Henri IV* is still something of a regional specialty though it has spread to other parts of France.

As you move a little further north, the woods provide wonderful mushrooms, especially *cèpes*, and ample and exotic game. Partridge, pheasant, woodcock, guineafowl, wild duck, wood pidgeon and ortolans appear on menus as frequently as hare, chicken, turkey and duck. But the goose is the national symbol of the Guyenne and the Gascogne, and strings of geese can be seen waddling down village streets and around every farmyard pond. Some are force-fed, to provide the huge distended livers for the *pâté de foie gras* for which the Perigord is world-famous. Goose is cooked a little differently wherever you go, according to local custom, but most often it is preserved in its own fat, and the *confit d'oie* adds a characteristic flavor to many dishes, such as the *garbure* of Béarn and the *cassoulet* of neighboring Languedoc. Goose fat is used instead of butter in much of the local cooking, even sometimes for baking, and the famous *beurre de Gascogne* is none other than goose fat mixed with large quantities of mashed garlic.

There are other specialties: the town of Moissac has its chasselas grapes, sold in the market square outside its incomparably lovely romanesque church; walnuts grow in huge quantities around Sarlat; Agen is famous for its plums, mostly dried to make prunes, some of which are stuffed with a sweet liqueur-flavored paste and sent around the world proudly proclaiming on their package "*je suis un pruneau d'Agen fourré*". But of course the most important specialty of the Perigord is the truffle, that highly prized "black diamond" which defies cultivation, and still needs trained pigs or dogs to snuffle it out, and which gives the *pâté de foie gras* of the Perigord its unique flavor, and, some would say, its supremacy over all other pâtés. Add to this the incomparable clarets from Bordeaux, Armagnac, the great brandy that is distilled in Gascony, the dessert wines from Monbazillac and the liqueurs from the Marie Brizard distilleries, and you have a gourmet's paradise.

Languedoc and Provence

These two Mediterranean provinces of France are like heavenly larders, so abundantly endowed are they by nature with glorious produce. The coastline provides the brilliantly colored, weirdly shaped fish of the Mediterranean: seabass, known as "wolf of the sea" (*loup de mer*), rosy mullet and silvery bream, fierce-looking rascasse and hideous gurnard, as well as sardines and shoals of anchovies. No wonder that the most famous dish from this part of France is the *bouillabaisse*, the great fish soup about whose precise correct contents aficionados argue interminably, the most fanatic among them claiming that the true *bouillabaisse* can only be obtained within sniffing distance of the port of Marseilles. Shellfish, from spiny lobsters (*langoustes*) and crabs, to clams, large and tiny, and sea-urchins, can also be enjoyed all along the coast, and especially in the restaurants and cafes of Sète and the little walled town of Aigues Mortes in the Camargue, that strange area of marshland, salt-pans, gray-blue skies, white horses and pink flamingos.

Provence has always had a magical quality, with its special light that has attracted painters as well as travelers, its groves of gnarled olive trees and its fragrant pinewoods which produce the pine kernels that are much used in provençal cooking, its herb-covered slopes and its cornucopia of vivid vegetables and fruit. The big, puckered, deep orange tomatoes have a taste that lingers in the memory and makes other tomatoes seem pallid in comparison; the eggplants seem a deeper purple here than elsewhere; the fennel is fat, crisp and pungent, and the artichokes tiny, spiny and flushed with violet. The special, wide-stemmed spinach is used in sweet as well as savory dishes, and the asparagus from Cavaillon is especially highly prized.

Cavaillon also produces some of the best melons – the astute Alexander Dumas once made a deal with the municipality of Cavaillon whereby he sent them a complete set of his more than four hundred works for their library in exchange for a life annuity of twelve Cavaillon melons a year, and hoped they found his books as charming as he found their fruit. The area around Carpentras and Avignon also grows wonderful peaches, pears, apricots, strawberries, cherries and even oranges and lemons, and nearby Apt has a flourishing candied fruit industry. No wonder that the bees of Provence produce such fragrant honey.

Olive oil and garlic are the predominant flavors of the provençal cuisine, and fruit and vegetables its greatest glory. As you move westwards into the Languedoc, the cooking changes to a more solid, earthbound style. Pork products become more evident, chestnuts and walnuts take over from almonds, and dried legumes are used a great deal. The little green and gray lentils from Le Puy are especially delicious, and further south, Toulouse, Carcassonne and Castelnaudary vie with each other as to which produces the best *cassoulet*, that marvelously sustaining dish of meat and beans.

As you get closer to the Pyrenees, the influence of Spanish cooking makes itself felt; a paella cooked in Toulouse will be as good as any you come across in Spain.

The Languedoc is also the home of one of the world's great cheeses, the Roquefort, mentioned by Pliny, praised by Charlemagne and appreciated by Rabelais. It is made in the Aveyron area only, from the milk of ewes that have grazed on the herb-scented grass of those uplands, and then matured in the natural caves of Roquefort itself. It is the chief pride and glory of the Languedoc.

Auvergne, Lyonnais, Savoie and Dauphiné

The Auvergne is in the heart of the Massif Central, the great central mountainous area of France. It is the country of Vercingetorix and the Arverni, a war-like tribe, and it is still a wild and barren area, romantically beautiful for the traveler, but relatively poor, for the land is hard to cultivate. Not surprisingly, the food tends to be good and simple country fare rather than haute cuisine. Potatoes and cabbage are the most popular vegetables, and lentils from Le Puy, a little further South, are also in demand.

As with other mountainous areas, the Auvergne is noted for its hams, raw and cooked, and sausages, and you will find an unusual variety of pork products in the local charcuteries. But if one had to choose one single characteristic food from these high pastures, it would be cheese. Cantal, made from cow's milk, is the best known. It has a long lineage, being first mentioned by Pliny the Elder two thousand years ago. It is not unlike a Cheddar or Brick cheese, and, like these, it is equally good to eat plain or for use in cooking. Indeed, there is a *soupe de Cantal* that is so thick with bread and cheese that you can stand a spoon in it. But there are many other varieties of cheese – some made from goat's milk, others from the milk of ewes. The Bleu d'Auvergne is made by the same method as Roquefort, but, being made from cow's milk, is considerably less expensive.

As so often in mountainous districts, the puddings tend to be as substantial as the main dishes, but the area around Clermont-Ferrand is a fertile fruit-growing valley, where there are not only a great many apple orchards, but cherries, apricots, strawberries and above all angelica are grown. This is a great center for making candied fruits and fruit pastes, while nearby Royat has a flourishing chocolate industry.

The Lyonnais is an altogether more prosperous region, and the Lyonnaises regard their city as the center of French gastronomy; certainly the area boasts an uncommon number of starred restaurants. Although a small region, it is blessed with the products of its neighbors – Burgundy is not far away, with its fine wines, its Charollais beef and chickens from Bresse. The fertile Rhône valley produces fruit and vegetables, notably onions, which are used so extensively in Lyonnaise cooking that the word on a menu is enough to imply that the dish contains onions. The truffles found in the area, while not as highly prized as those from the Perigord, are used in regional dishes, especially the famous *poulet demi-deuil*. Thin slices of truffle are slipped under the skin of the chicken breast before it is poached, giving it the appearance of being in half-mourning – a characteristically elaborate specialty of Lyons, and invented by the great Mère Fillioux, doyenne of Lyon's formidable army of women restaurateurs.

The Savoie and Dauphiné share borders along the Alps with Switzerland and Italy. This is an area of high mountains with inviting valleys, lakes and streams, and the cooking is simple, relying on the quality of the ingredients for its effects. There are fresh fish from the lakes and streams – carp, eel, pike and crayfish; the romantically named *ombre chevalier*, a kind of char, may be eaten here.

Cheeses are one of the chief products from the high alpine pastures, especially the dense Beaufort, used in fondue, and Reblochon, made near beautiful Lake Annecy.

The Dauphiné is also the home of Chartreuse, made to a sixteenth-century recipe from 130 aromatic plants and herbs that grow on the wooded slopes of the area.

Further south, in the Bas-Dauphiné, lies the town of Montélimar, devoted to the manufacture of nougat, made with almonds that have been grown in the area since almond trees were first planted there in the sixteenth century, and with the fragrant honey from Provence.

Soups

Potage Aux Moules *Mussel Soup*

BRITTANY

Mussels abound around the flat marshy Northern coastline of Brittany, and are served in numerous different ways, some more extravagant than others. This simple soup would be served piping hot from a fat tureen to start the family evening meal.

Preparation time: 20 minutes (plus cleaning mussels)
Cooking time: 15 minutes
To serve: 6

1 quart fresh mussels, cleaned
¾ cup white wine or cider
¼ cup butter
¼ cup flour
1 quart hot milk
pinch of cayenne
salt
freshly ground black pepper
pinch of saffron powder
2 tablespoons crème fraîche (see page 118)
    or heavy cream
1 egg yolk
1 tablespoon finely chopped fresh parsley

Put the mussels in a large saucepan with the wine or cider, cover the pan and cook over a high heat until the mussels open. Remove the mussels with a slotted spoon as soon as they open and take the meat from the shells. Discard any that do not open. Keep warm. Strain the liquid and reserve.

In a clean saucepan melt the butter, stir in the flour and cook over a gentle heat, without allowing to color, for 3 minutes. Remove from the heat and gradually stir in the strained mussel liquid. Stir until smooth, then slowly add the hot milk. Return to the heat and bring the soup to a boil. Stir in the cayenne, and salt and pepper to taste.

Mix the saffron and the crème fraîche with the egg yolk and add a little of the hot soup. Stir until smooth, then add to the rest of the soup together with the mussels. Heat through without allowing to boil. Sprinkle with the parsley before serving.

Potage Vert A La Creme *Cream of Artichoke Soup*

BRITTANY

Although globe artichokes grow to such fat and meaty perfection in the north of Brittany, you will rarely find them served here with the delicate sauces with which they appear in the richer parts of France. They may be served as an hors d'oeuvre with a simple vinaigrette, but more often they are used to flavor dishes such as this delicate and subtle soup.

Preparation time: 30 minutes
Cooking time: 30 minutes
To serve: 6 to 8

2 large globe artichokes
salt
¼ cup butter
2 potatoes, peeled and cubed
2 leeks, white parts only, thinly sliced
1 head of lettuce, leaves separated
1½ quarts chicken broth or water
1 egg yolk
¾ cup crème fraîche (see page 118)
freshly ground black pepper

Trim the tips of the leaves using kitchen scissors. Plunge the artichokes into boiling salted water and cook until just tender. Drain. When cool enough to handle, remove the leaves and hairy choke. Roughly chop the hearts.

Melt the butter in a large saucepan, add the potatoes and leeks, cover and cook gently for 5 minutes to soften. Add the lettuce leaves and the chopped artichoke hearts. Stir in the broth or water. Bring to a boil and simmer for 20 minutes or until all the vegetables are quite tender.

Pass the soup through a blender or food processor, and then through a nylon sieve to remove any fibers. Return to a clean pan and bring back to a boil.

Mix the egg yolk with the crème fraîche. Take the soup off the heat and add the cream mixture. Return to the heat and heat through without allowing to boil, stirring well. Add salt and pepper to taste and serve.

Soupe à La Bretonne *Navy Bean Soup*

BRIT...

A re... it on
a c...

Pre... king
Co... To... in the

1 c... r

$\frac{1}{4}$ ...
2 ...
2 ...
2 ...
2 ... a good

1 ... and

s...
f...
1 ... *sley*

Drain and rinse the beans. Put them in a saucepan, cover with fresh cold water and bring to a boil. Drain and rinse again.

Melt half the butter in a large saucepan, add the onions and leeks and fry over a gentle heat until softened. Add the tomatoes and beans, then add the broth, or the water and bone, and the bouquet garni. Bring to a boil, then cover and simmer for at least 1 hour or until the beans are tender. If they are not fresh, they may take considerably longer to cook.

When the beans are quite soft, remove the bouquet garni and bone, if used, and pass the soup through a blender or food processor. Return the soup to the pan and reheat gently. Add salt and pepper, then stir in the remaining butter, cut into small pieces, to give the soup a glaze. Sprinkle with the parsley and serve.

Potage vert à la crème and potage aux moules

15

Crème Dieppoise *Cream of Fish and Mussel Soup*

NORMANDY

This soup is almost a meal in itself, and though it is rich, and requires several processes to make, it is not expensive and is well worth the effort. White fish, such as cod is excellent. Serve with crusty French bread, and follow with a light omelette or salad.

Preparation time: 40 minutes (plus cleaning mussels)
Cooking time: 50 minutes
To serve: 6 to 8

1 lb filleted white fish, and about ½ lb of the fish bones, heads or trimmings reserved
dash of wine vinegar
1 quart fresh mussels, cleaned
1¼ cups wine or cider
6 tablespoons butter
2 onions, finely chopped
1 carrot, finely chopped
2 large leeks, white parts only, finely chopped
2 celery stalks, finely chopped
1 cup finely chopped white mushrooms
1 tablespoon flour
1 bay leaf
1 parsley sprig
salt
freshly ground black pepper
¾ cup crème fraîche (see page 118)
1 egg yolk
1 tablespoon finely chopped fresh parsley

Put the fish bones and trimmings in a saucepan, add the vinegar and cover with cold water. Bring to a boil and simmer for 20 minutes. Strain the stock and make it up to 1 quart with water.

Put the mussels in a large saucepan with the wine or cider, cover the pan and cook over a high heat until the mussels open. Remove the mussels with a slotted spoon as soon as they open, take the meat from the shells and set aside. Discard any mussels that remain closed. Strain the cooking liquid and reserve.

Melt ¼ cup of the butter in a large saucepan, add the vegetables and cook gently until they are soft, but not browned. Sprinkle with the flour, stir well and continue to cook over a low heat for 3 minutes, without allowing to brown.

Add the fish, fish stock, bay leaf and parsley and bring to a boil, stirring well. Cover and simmer for 5 to 10 minutes or until the fish is tender.

Remove the bay leaf and parsley, then blend or pass through a food processor. Return the soup to a clean saucepan and stir in the cooking liquid from the mussels and salt and pepper to taste. Bring to a boil. Remove from the heat and stir in the crème fraîche mixed with the egg yolk, followed by the mussels and the remaining butter cut into small pieces. Heat through gently without allowing to boil. Sprinkle with the parsley and serve.

Potage Crécy *Carrot Soup*

ILE-DE-FRANCE

Some of the best carrots come from the area around Crécy, east of Paris, so this light and delicately colored soup takes its name from there.

Preparation time: 20 minutes
Cooking time: 30 to 40 minutes
To serve: 6

½ cup butter
1 lb carrots, sliced
1 medium-size onion, finely chopped
½ teaspoon sugar
salt
freshly ground black pepper
⅓ cup long-grain rice
1 quart hot chicken or veal broth
2 parsley sprigs
2 slices of stale white bread, cubed

Melt half the butter in a heavy saucepan and add the carrots, onion, sugar and salt and pepper to taste. Cover and cook over a gentle heat for 10 minutes.

Add the rice and stir well, then pour on the hot broth. Add the parsley sprigs. Bring to a boil, cover and simmer for 20 minutes, or until the vegetables and the rice are quite soft.

Remove the parsley sprigs and pass the soup through a blender or food processor, and then through a nylon sieve. Return to a clean saucepan, adjust the seasoning and heat through.

Melt 3 tablespoons of the remaining butter in a skillet and fry the cubes of bread until they are crisp and golden brown. Drain on paper towels.

Cut the remaining butter into small pieces, add to the soup to give it a glaze. Serve very hot, with the croûtons served separately.

Potage Normande *Fish Soup with Shrimp*

NORMANDY

This soup looks deceptively bland but it has a richly fishy flavor.

Preparation time: 25 minutes
Cooking time: 20 minutes
To serve: 6

1 pint cooked shrimp in their shells
½ lb filleted fish, bones reserved
¾ cup white wine or cider
1 quart water
1 bouquet garni
2 tablespoons butter
1 onion, finely chopped
1 carrot, finely chopped
1 celery stalk, finely chopped
1 cup soft white bread crumbs
pinch of saffron powder
juice of ½ lemon or to taste
salt
freshly ground black pepper
¾ cup crème fraîche (see page 118)
1 egg yolk
1 tablespoon finely chopped fresh parsley

Peel and devein the shrimp, reserving the shells. Put the fish bones and shrimp shells into a saucepan, add the wine or cider, water and bouquet garni and bring to a boil. Simmer for 20 minutes. Strain the stock.

Melt the butter in a large saucepan, add the vegetables and cook without stirring for 5 minutes. Add the fish and cook very gently until tender.

Put the fish mixture, shrimp and bread crumbs into a blender or food processor together with a little of the fish stock and blend until smooth. Return to the saucepan and add the remaining fish stock, saffron, lemon juice and salt and pepper to taste. Bring to a boil, stirring occasionally. Stir in the crème fraîche mixed with the egg yolk and heat through without allowing to boil. Adjust the seasoning, sprinkle with the parsley and serve.

Soupe A L'Oignon *Onion Soup*

PARIS

One of the best known of French soups, this used to be served, piping hot and well laced with Cognac, in the early hours of the morning in Les Halles, when this was still the central market of Paris. Though the soup itself is quite thin, it is warming and very sustaining. The cheese croûte gradually gets softened and impregnated with the soup as you pull it down into the bowl to cut off a piece with each spoonful.

Preparation time: 30 minutes
Cooking time: 45 minutes
To serve: 6

¼ cup butter
1 tablespoon oil
1 lb onions, thinly sliced
½ teaspoon sugar
1 tablespoon flour
1 quart beef broth
salt
freshly ground black pepper
6 slices of stale French bread
1 garlic clove, halved
1 cup shredded Gruyère or Swiss cheese
2 tablespoons brandy (optional)

Melt the butter with the oil in a large heavy saucepan and add the onions. Stir well. Cover and cook over a moderate heat for 20 minutes, or until the onions are quite soft and butter yellow. Raise the heat, sprinkle on the sugar and cook, uncovered and stirring frequently, until the onions turn a rich golden brown.

Sprinkle with the flour and when this has also browned, add the broth and salt and pepper to taste. Stir well. Bring to a boil, cover and simmer for a further 20 minutes.

Meanwhile, rub the slices of bread with the cut surface of the clove of garlic. Dry or toast gently under the broiler. Pile a little of the cheese on each slice and melt under the broiler until lightly browned.

When the soup is ready, adjust the seasoning and add the brandy, if used. Pour into individual bowls and float a cheese croûte in each bowl.

La Potée   *Bacon and Vegetable Soup*

PICARDY

A cross between a soup and a stew, rather like a pot-au-feu, this is a real peasant dish, which can be eaten all in one, or served in two courses, with the broth followed by the meat and vegetables. The vegetable ingredients do not have to be exact, and the country housewife would simply use whatever vegetables are at hand.

Preparation time: 15 minutes
Cooking time: about 2 hours
To serve: 6 to 8

*about 2 lb slab bacon, soaked overnight if
    very salty and drained*
2 leeks
1 bouquet garni
6 to 8 carrots, peeled or scraped
6 to 8 medium-size potatoes, peeled
6 to 8 small onions, peeled
*1 small cabbage, quartered, cored, blanched
    and shredded*
2 cups shelled peas or lima beans
salt
freshly ground black pepper
*2 to 3 slices of thick wholewheat bread
    (optional)*

Put the bacon into a very large saucepan or Dutch oven, cover with fresh water and bring to a boil. Boil gently for 10 minutes, then throw away the water.

Rinse the bacon and the pan and cover again with at least 2 quarts cold water. Bring to a boil, add the leeks and bouquet garni and simmer for 1 hour. Add the carrots, potatoes and onions and simmer for a further 30 minutes.

Remove the leeks and the bouquet garni. Add the cabbage and peas or beans and simmer for another 10 to 15 minutes, or until the green vegetables are cooked.

Remove the piece of bacon to a heated serving dish, and surround with the vegetables.

Taste the broth for seasoning; add a little salt if necessary and some pepper. If the soup is to be served separately, it is often poured onto some thick slices of wholewheat bread for serving.

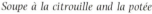

Soupe à la citrouille and la potée

Soupe A La Citrouille *Pumpkin Soup*

PICARDY

If you are making a large quantity of this soup, the prettiest way to serve it is to use a whole or a half pumpkin. Hollow out the pumpkin carefully, and serve the soup in the shell.

Preparation time: 15 minutes
Cooking time: 20 minutes
To serve: 6

2 lb pumpkin, peeled, seeded and cubed
1 onion, peeled
3 cloves
1 quart milk
2½ cups broth or water
1 bay leaf
salt
freshly ground black pepper
¼ cup butter
1 thick slice of stale white bread, cubed
1 tablespoon crème fraîche (see page 118),
  (optional)

Put the pumpkin cubes into a large saucepan with the onion stuck with the cloves, the milk, broth or water, bay leaf and salt and pepper to taste. Bring to a boil and simmer until the pumpkin is very tender.

Remove the cloves and bay leaf. Put the soup through a blender or food processor and then through a fine sieve. Return to the clean saucepan, reheat and adjust the seasoning.

Meanwhile melt all but 1 tablespoon of the butter in a skillet. When foaming add the cubes of bread and fry until golden brown on all sides. Drain on paper towels.

Stir the reserved butter into the soup to give it a glaze, swirl in the crème fraîche, if used, and scatter on the croûtons just before serving.

La Chaudrée Charentaise *Fish Chowder*

CHARENTE

The American word "chowder" derives from the *chaudrées* of the Atlantic coast of France, where fish soups or stews are cooked in tall *chaudrons* or cauldrons. An assortment of sea fish, such as sole, hake, flounder, cod or whiting would be used, as well as eel and even sometimes carp.

Preparation time: 20 minutes
Cooking time: 35 to 40 minutes
To serve: 6

½ cup butter
12 small onions, peeled
12 medium-size potatoes, peeled
salt
freshly ground black pepper
2 to 2¼ lb assorted firm fish (see above),
  cleaned and cut into large chunks or
  filleted
1 bouquet garni
1 quart white wine
6 slices of stale white bread
1 garlic clove, halved
1 tablespoon oil
1 tablespoon finely chopped fresh parsley

Melt 2 tablespoons of the butter in a heavy flameproof casserole or cauldron. Put in the onions, lay the potatoes on top, dot them with another 2 tablespoons of the butter and season generously with salt and pepper. Lay the fish on top of the potatoes, starting with the firmest fish and ending with the softest. Put the bouquet garni on top.

Bring the wine to a boil in a separate saucepan and pour into the casserole. Cover and simmer for about 30 minutes.

Meanwhile, rub the slices of bread on both sides with the cut surface of the clove of garlic. Melt half the remaining butter with the oil in a skillet and quickly fry the bread until it is golden brown on both sides. Drain on paper towels.

Remove the pieces of fish to a heated serving tureen as they are cooked, and keep warm. When all the fish and the potatoes are done and have been transferred to the tureen, raise the heat and bring the liquid to a boil. Boil fiercely to reduce for 5 minutes.

Remove from the heat, add the remaining butter cut into small pieces and pour into the tureen. Sprinkle with the parsley and serve hot.

Serve the fried bread separately, allowing everyone to put a slice into their bowls before adding the soup.

Soupe A La Savoyarde *Celeriac Soup*

SAVOIE

A sustaining soup, this has a very subtle flavor.

Preparation time: 10 minutes
Cooking time: 30 minutes
To serve: 6

$\frac{1}{4}$ *cup butter*
1 large celeriac (about $\frac{3}{4}$ lb), peeled and
  diced
1 onion, finely chopped
1 large potato, peeled and diced
1 quart chicken broth
salt
freshly ground black pepper
1 cup milk
1 tablespoon finely chopped fresh parsley

Melt the butter in a large heavy saucepan, add the vegetables, cover and cook very gently for 10 minutes to soften, without allowing them to brown.

Add the broth and salt and pepper to taste and bring to a boil. Simmer until the vegetables are tender. Put through a blender or food processor and return to the clean saucepan.

Stir in the milk and bring to a boil. Adjust the seasoning, adding plenty of pepper to counteract the slight sweetness of the celeriac. Sprinkle with the parsley before serving.

Potée Au Chou Savoyarde *Pork and Vegetable Soup*

SAVOIE

More like a stew than a soup, this is a meal in itself, economical and satisfying.

Preparation time: 20 minutes
Cooking time: $2\frac{1}{2}$ hours
To serve: 6 to 8

$\frac{1}{4}$ *cup lard*
1 lb lean boneless pork
$\frac{1}{2}$ *lb salt pork, soaked in cold water*
  overnight
1 lb carrots, halved or quartered
2 leeks, finely chopped
1 lb turnips, peeled if necessary and halved
1 bouquet garni
2 garlic cloves, peeled
4 cloves
1$\frac{1}{2}$ lb potatoes, peeled and halved or quartered
2 onions, quartered
1 large boiling sausage
1 savoy cabbage, quartered and cored
salt
freshly ground black pepper

Melt the lard in a very large saucepan and quickly brown both pieces of pork on all sides. Add the carrots, leeks and turnips, cover with cold water and add the bouquet garni and the cloves of garlic stuck with the cloves. Bring slowly to a boil. Simmer for about 1 hour.

Add the potatoes, onions and the sausage, well-pricked with a fork, and continue to simmer for another hour.

Blanch the cabbage in boiling salted water for 2 minutes, then drain and add to the pot. Simmer for a further 30 minutes.

Adjust the seasoning and remove the bouquet garni before serving.

La Garbure Béarnaise *Vegetable and Meat Soup*

BEARN

An age-old country soup, this is a hefty meal in itself. It belongs to the mountainous region of the Pyrenees, where the weather can be very raw, and goose, and especially goose fat, is used a good deal to provide internal insulation. When this is not available, pork and pork fat may be used instead. The custom of *faire chabrol* is associated with this soup – a glass of wine is added to the remaining broth in each bowl after all the meat and vegetables have been eaten.

Preparation time: 40 minutes
Cooking time: 2½ hours
To serve: 8 minimum

½ lb slab bacon
1 piece of preserved goose, or ½ lb piece of
    smoked pork
1 celery stalk
6 garlic cloves, lightly crushed
1 large onion, peeled
2 cloves
1 bouquet garni
salt
freshly ground black pepper
4 large potatoes, peeled and cubed
1 turnip, diced
2 leeks, sliced
4 carrots, diced
2 cups shelled lima beans
2 cups shelled peas
1 small cabbage, cored and shredded
8 slices of strong country bread

Put the pieces of bacon and goose or pork into a very large saucepan and cook gently until the fat begins to run. Remove the piece of goose, but leave the pork.

Add the celery, garlic, the onion stuck with the cloves and the bouquet garni and cover with as much cold water as the saucepan will hold (3½ quarts would not be too much, but add as much as you can and replenish when possible during the cooking time). Season liberally and bring slowly to a boil. Keep at a steady simmer for 30 minutes, then add the potatoes, turnip, leeks and carrots and cook for another hour.

Add the beans and peas. When the soup has simmered for another 30 minutes add the cabbage and return the goose, if used, to the pot. Cook for at least a further 30 minutes.

Take out the pieces of meat and cut into chunks. Return these to the pot. Adjust the seasoning. Put a slice of bread in each soup bowl and pour the soup over to serve.

Potage Purée Des Petits Pois Frais St. Germain

Smooth Green Pea Soup St. Germain style

ILE DE FRANCE

St. Germain is the student quarter of Paris, the famous "Left Bank." But this delicate, elegant soup is more at home in the salons of the well-off intellectuals of the precinct.

Preparation time: 30 minutes
Cooking time: 30 minutes
To serve: 6

4 cups shelled green peas
salt
¼ cup butter
1½ quarts chicken broth
¾ cup heavy cream
chopped fresh chervil to garnish

Cook the peas in a minimum of boiling salted water for 10–15 minutes until tender. Drain and reserve 2 tablespoons of the peas. Return the remainder to a large saucepan and sauté gently in the butter for a few minutes. Add the chicken broth and bring to a boil. Lower the heat and simmer for 10 minutes.

Remove the saucepan from the heat, and put the soup a little at a time through a blender or food processor. Return the pea purée to the saucepan and simmer, while adding the cream. Sprinkle with the reserved peas and cook for 1 minute. Serve the soup in heated bowls and scatter chopped chervil on top.

Crème Vichyssoise *Leek and Potato Soup*

BOURBONNAIS

This delicate and pretty summer soup takes its name from the elegant spa town of Vichy which was the home of its inventor. It is a relative newcomer and does not really belong to traditional French cooking, but it is too good to omit.

Preparation time: 20 minutes
Cooking time: 20 minutes
To serve: 4 to 6

2 tablespoons butter
2 lb leeks, white parts only, chopped
½ lb potatoes, peeled and diced
1 quart chicken or veal broth
salt
white pepper
1 cup light cream
2 tablespoons chopped fresh chives

Melt the butter in a large saucepan, add the leeks and potatoes and soften, stirring well so that they become evenly coated with butter. Add the broth and salt and pepper to taste, bring to a boil and simmer until the vegetables are quite tender.

Put through a blender or food processor until smooth and chill.

Just before serving, stir in the cream, adjust the seasoning and sprinkle with the chopped chives.

Soupe A L'Oseille *Sorrel Soup*

BURGUNDY

Sorrel, with its long red stalks and pointed green acid leaves, grows wild in many country districts in central France, as well as in kitchen gardens, and makes this lovely light and simple refreshing soup.

Preparation time: 10 minutes
Cooking time: 15 minutes
To serve: 6

¼ cup butter
1 large onion, finely chopped
1 potato, peeled and diced
½ lb sorrel leaves, stripped of the thicker
  stalks
1½ quarts chicken broth
salt
freshly ground black pepper
¾ cup cream
2 egg yolks

Melt 3 tablespoons of the butter in a large heavy saucepan, add the onion and potato and fry until the onion is softened. Add the sorrel leaves and cook, stirring, over a moderate heat for a few minutes until the sorrel has wilted. Add the broth and cook for a further 5 minutes. Season to taste with salt and pepper.

Stir the cream into the egg yolks to make a smooth mixture, then add a little of the soup and stir until smooth. Add to the remaining soup and heat, stirring, over a moderate heat; do not allow to boil. Adjust the seasoning and add the remaining butter, a little at a time, to give the soup a glaze. Serve hot.

Soupe à l'oseille, crème Vichyssoise and soupe aux mousserons

Soupe Aux Mousserons *Mushroom Soup*

BURGUNDY

Made with full-flavored field mushrooms, or *mousserons des près*, this is a fine soup, light but with a full flavor. If cultivated mushrooms have to be used, double the quantity.

Preparation time: 15 minutes
Cooking time: 30 minutes
To serve: 4 to 6

¼ *cup butter*
1 onion, finely chopped
2 cups roughly chopped mushrooms
1 tablespoon flour
1½ quarts hot chicken or veal broth
4 slices of French bread
½ *cup grated Gruyère or Comté cheese*
salt
freshly ground black pepper
pinch of grated nutmeg
2 tablespoons crème fraîche (see page 118)
*   or light cream*
1 tablespoon chopped fresh parsley

Melt the butter in a large heavy saucepan, add the onion and fry until lightly colored. Add the mushrooms and cook just until they begin to give out their moisture. Sprinkle on the flour and cook, stirring, for 2 minutes, without allowing to brown. Stir in the broth until smooth. Bring to a boil, then simmer for 15 minutes.

Meanwhile, toast the slices of bread lightly and put them in the bottom of a heated soup tureen. Sprinkle with the cheese and keep warm.

Blend the soup very briefly – it should not be completely smooth but should be quite a thin soup with small pieces of mushrooms in it. Reheat and season to taste with salt and pepper and the nutmeg. Bring just to a boil, then pour over the bread in the tureen and leave to soak for a few minutes.

Add a swirl of cream and sprinkle with parsley before serving.

Soupe Gratinée Lyonnaise *Cheese and Onion Soup*

LYONNAIS

The Auvergne has a *soupe de Cantal*, an onion and cheese soup which is so dense that you can stand a spoon in it. This is a lighter version, to be made with Cantal or Gruyère cheese.

Preparation time: 20 minutes
Cooking time: 1 hour
Oven temperature: 425°
To serve: 6

½ cup butter
1 lb onions, finely chopped
¼ cup flour
pinch of dried mixed herbs
salt
freshly ground black pepper
1 quart water
6 slices of French bread
1½ cups shredded Cantal or Gruyère cheese
2 egg yolks
1 tablespoon brandy or marc

Melt the butter in a large heavy saucepan and add the onions. Cover and cook over a moderate heat until the onions are almost melted and golden yellow. They must not be allowed to brown.

Sprinkle on the flour, stir well and cook for a further 2 minutes. Add the herbs and salt and pepper to taste, then slowly stir in the water. Bring to a boil, cover and simmer for at least 30 minutes. Put the soup through a blender or food processor and adjust the seasoning.

Dry out the pieces of bread in the oven or toast them quite lightly. Place them in an ovenproof tureen, sprinkle on half the cheese and pour on the soup. Sprinkle the remaining cheese on top. Place the tureen in the oven and heat for 10 to 15 minutes or until the cheese has melted and begins to form a crust.

Whisk the egg yolks with the brandy and pour into the soup. Give a good stir and serve very hot.

Soupe Au Lait Aux Oignons *Onion and Milk Soup*

LORRAINE

This is a really warming and sustaining, but delicately flavored soup.

Preparation time: 15 minutes
Cooking time: 40 minutes
To serve: 6 to 8

½ cup butter
1 lb onions, finely chopped
salt
freshly ground black pepper
⅛ teaspoon grated nutmeg
2½ cups chicken broth
1 quart milk
4 slices of stale white bread, cubed
1 egg yolk
2 tablespoons crème fraîche (see page 118)
  or heavy cream

Melt half the butter in a large, heavy saucepan and add the onions. Season with salt, pepper and nutmeg, cover and soften for about 10 minutes, without allowing the onions to brown. They should be a rich buttery yellow.

Add the chicken broth, bring to a boil and simmer, uncovered, for 20 minutes, so that the broth becomes reduced to half its original quantity.

Put the soup through a blender or food processor. If the onions have been very finely chopped, you may wish to omit this step. Return to the saucepan, add the milk and simmer for another 10 minutes.

Melt the remaining butter in a skillet and quickly fry the bread cubes until they are golden brown. Drain on paper towels.

Stir the egg yolk and cream together. Add a little of the soup and stir to make a smooth sauce. Pour into the remaining soup, stir well and adjust the seasoning. Serve the soup very hot, adding the croûtons of bread at the last minute.

Hors d'Oeuvre, Pâtés and Salads

Galantine De Canard

Duck Pâté
NORMANDY

The *charcuteries* of Rouen are a delight and their windows as enticing to the eye as a toy store. There are rabbit pâtés molded into rabbit shapes, and duck pâtés molded into ducks, as well as a wonderful selection of terrines in casseroles shaped as nesting pheasants, venison rampant, and rabbits couchant. This duck pâté, though it requires some skill in boning the duck – or a butcher willing to do it for you – is not difficult to make, and is rich and delicious as well as looking impressive. Keep the carcass for stock.

Preparation time: about 40 minutes (plus marinating and setting)
Cooking time: 1½ hours
Oven temperature: 350°
To serve: 10 to 12

1 dressed duck, boned, giblets reserved
2 to 3 extra duck or chicken livers (optional)
2 to 3 shallots, halved
strip of orange rind
pinch of ground allspice
1 fresh thyme branch
2 bay leaves
salt
freshly ground black pepper
3 tablespoons Calvados
2 tablespoons butter
6 to 8 shallots, finely chopped
½ lb ground lean pork (about 1 cup)
½ lb ground pork fat (about 1 cup)
½ lb ground veal (about 1 cup)
1 egg
3 to 4 strips of pork fat or bacon

Galantine de canard

Cut off as much meat from the duck after boning as is possible without damaging the skin. Cut the meat into strips and place in a bowl. Add the giblet meat and livers, also cut into large strips, the halved shallots, orange rind, allspice, thyme, 1 bay leaf and salt and pepper to taste. Sprinkle on the Calvados and leave to marinate overnight, or at least for a few hours. Strain off the marinating liquid and reserve.

Melt the butter in a skillet, add the chopped shallots and cook until golden brown. Combine the ground meats well in a bowl and add the cooked shallots and the egg beaten with the strained marinating liquid. Mix well together and add salt and pepper to taste. (It is worth cooking a small pat of the forcemeat in a little butter to get the seasoning right.)

Spread the duck skin flat on a working surface, outside down. Put half the forcemeat into the center and flatten the surface. Make a layer of the duck meat and liver mixture on top and cover with the remaining forcemeat. Pat into a rounded shape. Wrap the sides of the duck skin right around and sew it up, first down the center and then all the other openings.

Season the outside of the duck package lightly and place in an oval terrine of the right size. Cover the top with the second bay leaf and the strips of pork fat or bacon. Cook in the oven for 1½ hours, or until the juice that comes out, when the pâté is pricked with a skewer, is just clear.

Place a piece of buttered wax paper, butter side down, over the pâté, put a board on top and then add a heavy weight to press the pâté down. Leave overnight to set and to allow the flavor to mature. You can serve the galantine from the terrine, or you may unmold it before serving.

Hors D'Oeuvre Aux Crevettes

Shrimp Appetizer
NORMANDY

A substantial and refreshing hors d'oeuvre, this can be made with small or jumbo shrimp.

Preparation time: 15 minutes
To serve: 4

1 small head of lettuce, leaves separated
2 apples, cored and chopped
$\frac{1}{4}$ lb cooked shrimp, shelled and deveined
1 cup roughly chopped walnuts
large squeeze of lemon juice
salt and freshly ground black pepper
$\frac{1}{2}$ teaspoon Dijon-style mustard
2 tablespoons crème fraîche (see page 118)
　or heavy cream

Line a salad bowl with the lettuce leaves. In another bowl, mix together the apples, shrimp and walnuts and sprinkle with the lemon juice. Season to taste with salt and pepper. Stir the mustard into the crème fraîche, season again and fold into the apple, shrimp and walnut mixture. Spoon into the center of the salad bowl and serve.

Hors d'oeuvre aux crevettes

Omelette Poularde *Soufflé Omelette*

NORMANDY

This is a specialty of La Mère Poularde, proprietor of the famous restaurant that nestles at the foot of Mont St. Michel. There the omelette is served between the fish and meat course, but it may well be served as a simple lunch or supper dish.
Fresh eggs are essential for this dish.

Preparation time: 5 minutes
Cooking time: 5 to 8 minutes
To serve: 1

2 fresh eggs, separated
salt
freshly ground black pepper
1 tablespoon butter

Beat the egg yolks lightly with salt and pepper to taste. Beat the whites until they stand in peaks but are not quite dry. Fold them into the yolks. Heat the omelette pan over a high heat, then lower the heat and put in the butter. Swirl the butter around the pan. When the butter is sizzling but has not changed color, pour in the omelette mixture.

Shake the pan a little, and as the omelette begins to set, scrape the bottom of the pan gently with a fork, and run a spatula around the edges. As soon as the bottom of the omelette has become golden brown and slightly crisp, slip the spatula underneath and fold the omelette in half. Slide onto a heated plate and serve.

Salade Cauchoise *Potato, Celery and Ham Salad*

NORMANDY

A nourishing salad, serve it for lunch or after a light main course.

Preparation time: 10 minutes
Cooking time: 15 minutes
To serve: 4

1 lb new or waxy potatoes
1 large head of celery, trimmed and cut into thin strips
salt
freshly ground black pepper
2 tablespoons wine vinegar
1 cup crème fraîche (see page 118)
¼ lb cooked ham, cut into thin strips
½ tablespoon finely chopped fresh parsley

Cook the potatoes in their skins in boiling water until just tender. Drain, then peel while still hot. Cut into thin strips. Mix the celery gently with the potato and season generously with salt and pepper. Sprinkle on the vinegar and cool.

Whip the cream lightly and fold into the potato mixture. Sprinkle with the ham and parsley and serve.

Salade Aux Moules *Mussel Salad*

ARTOIS

A tasty fish salad, serve this as a rather substantial hors d'oeuvre.

Preparation time: 20 minutes (plus cleaning of mussels)
Cooking time: 30 minutes
To serve: 6

2 quarts fresh mussels, cleaned
¾ cup white wine
1 small onion, finely chopped
1 bouquet garni
1 lb new potatoes
1 quantity sauce vinaigrette (see page 110)
1 tablespoon chopped fresh chives

Put the mussels in a large saucepan with the wine, onion and bouquet garni. Cover the pan and cook over a high heat until the mussels open, shaking the pan from time to time so that the mussels cook evenly. Remove the mussels with a slotted spoon as soon as they open, take the meat from the shells and set aside. Discard any mussels that remain closed. Strain the cooking liquid and reserve.

Cook the potatoes in their skins in boiling water until just tender. Drain and, as soon as they are cool enough to handle, peel and slice them quickly. Sprinkle 2 or 3 tablespoons of the strained mussel liquid over the potatoes, stir in the vinaigrette, add the mussels and turn well. Leave to cool.

Sprinkle with the chives before serving.

Les Betteraves Au Four Baked Beets

PICARDY

Beets are mostly served hot, and usually on their own, so that their color does not contaminate other food, and their full flavor, which is beautifully preserved by this cooking method, can be appreciated. Use small young beets, very fresh.

Preparation time: 10 minutes
Cooking time: 45 minutes to 1 hour
Oven temperature: 375°
To serve: 4

1 lb beets
1 tablespoon butter
squeeze of lemon juice
salt
freshly ground black pepper

Wash the beets but do not peel them. Cut the stalk off well above the root, to prevent bleeding. Put the whole beets into a well-buttered baking dish and bake until tender.

When they are cooked, remove from the oven and peel. Quarter or slice the beets, return to the dish and add the squeeze of lemon juice and salt and pepper to taste. Heat through before serving.

Rillettes De Porc Potted Pork

TOURAINE

The *charcuteries* and market stalls of the Touraine are full of stoneware pots of all sizes, sometimes covered with a pretty piece of gingham, containing rillettes de porc, for the district prides itself on making this preserve better than any other area of France. In spite of modern methods of refrigeration, this old farmhouse method of rendering down and preserving in fat is still used to make tasty *confits* of all kinds. Rillettes de porc are easy to make, keep well in the refrigerator for several weeks, and may be eaten cold as an hors d'oeuvre with mustard, or warmed, with mashed potatoes.

Preparation time: 30 minutes
Cooking time: 6 hours
To serve: 4 to 8

2 lb fresh pork sides, skinned, boned and cut into 1 inch cubes
1 teaspoon salt
$\frac{1}{2}$ teaspoon coarsely ground black pepper
1 bouquet garni (bay leaf and thyme and rosemary sprigs)
$\frac{1}{8}$ teaspoon ground allspice
$\frac{1}{4}$ teaspoon grated nutmeg
$\frac{1}{4}$ teaspoon ground cinnamon
$\frac{1}{4}$ teaspoon ground cloves
$\frac{1}{4}$ cup lard (optional)

Put all the ingredients, except the lard, into a very heavy pan, wide enough, if possible, to allow all the meat to touch the bottom of the pan. Add just enough water to stop the meat from burning, cover the pan and melt over a very, very low heat for about 6 hours. Stir from time to time and add a little more water if necessary. The meat should become quite soft, but not totally disintegrated, and it must not be allowed to brown.

Strain off the liquid into a bowl and chill it in order to let the fat set. Put the meat into a large bowl. Remove the bouquet garni. Pound the meat with a wooden spoon or mallet, then pull it into threads with two forks. The mixture should become light and thready. You can process the meat briefly in small batches in a blender, but do not use a food processor.

Taste for seasoning; if underseasoned, return the meat to the cooking pot and add more seasoning to taste. Heat through to distribute the seasoning evenly.

Divide the meat mixture between prepared sterilized pots, preferably stoneware; glass canning jars will also do. Gently warm the fat until just runny, then pour enough of it over the top of the pots to make a $\frac{1}{2}$ inch layer. Be careful not to include any of the meat juice that will have settled at the bottom of the bowl. If there is not enough fat, you may have to use some lard. Refrigerate overnight.

The next day, cover the pots with plastic wrap and foil, or gingham, and tie on securely. If you are eating the rillettes cold, do not serve straight from the refrigerator, but allow at least 1 hour at room temperature before serving.

Salade De Pommes De Terre Parisienne *Potato Salad*

ILE DE FRANCE

This delicate potato salad must be made with waxy new potatoes that will keep their shape. It is excellent served plain, and even more delicious when some champignons de Paris, the slightly brown-tinged button mushrooms, are folded in gently just before serving.

Preparation time: 15 minutes
Cooking time: 15 to 20 minutes
To serve: 6

2 lb new potatoes
1¼ cups white wine
1 tablespoon wine vinegar
3 tablespoons corn or nut oil
salt
freshly ground black pepper
½ lb button mushrooms, thinly sliced and
    sprinkled with lemon juice (optional)
½ tablespoon finely chopped fresh parsley,
    chives or tarragon

Cook the potatoes in their skins in boiling water until they are just tender. Drain and peel them carefully. Slice fairly thinly into a bowl containing the wine. Turn once gently and leave to cool.

When the potatoes are cold, sprinkle on the vinegar, oil and salt and pepper to taste and turn very gently, being careful not to break the potatoes. Gently fold in the mushrooms, if used.

Sprinkle with the herbs just before serving.

Les Asperges *Asparagus*

ILE DE FRANCE

Asparagus is grown in many parts of France, but some of the best still comes from Argenteuil, on the outskirts of Paris. It is not quite as fat and white nor as highly prized as the asparagus of Cavaillon, but has a slightly green tinge and excellent flavor. There are many different ways of serving asparagus – cold, with a vinaigrette (see page 110) or mayonnaise – or hot, simply with melted butter, or, more elaborately, with a beurre blanc (see page 112), a sauce hollandaise (see page 113) or a sauce mousseline (see page 110). But the first consideration is to cook it well.

Preparation time: 10 minutes
Cooking time: 12 to 20 minutes
To serve: 2 to 3

1 lb asparagus
salt

Take each asparagus spear individually, and hold it tip downwards. Using a small sharp kitchen knife, cut off any solidly wooden part at the bottom, then pare or shave off the tough outer skin, from the bottom upwards, as far as necessary.

Tie the spears into convenient bundles, tying them twice, near the top and near the bottom. If you do not have a special asparagus pan, use a skillet large enough to hold the bundles lying flat and lower them into boiling salted water. Bring back to a boil and boil steadily until the bottom ends of the asparagus are tender when tested with the sharp point of a knife. Lift out the bundles and drain.

Les asperges, salade de champignons à la crème (page 37)
and salade de pommes de terre Parisienne

Les Oeufs A L'Auvergnate *Eggs Baked with Cheese and Cream*

AUVERGNE

This delicate dish is made in Auvergne with the local Cantal cheese, a hard pressed cheese made from cow's milk. A Gruyère would be the nearest alternative. Serve one egg per person as an appetizer, two for a light main course.

Preparation time: 15 minutes
Cooking time: 10 minutes
Oven temperature: 350°
To serve: 4 to 8

8 eggs, separated
salt
freshly ground black pepper
1 tablespoon butter
¼ cup crème fraîche (see page 118) or
*   heavy cream*
¾ cup shredded Cantal or Gruyère cheese

Season the egg whites with salt and pepper and beat them until stiff and dry.

Butter a large tube pan generously and spoon in the egg whites evenly, smoothing the top. Make eight indentations with the back of a soup spoon at regular intervals and drop one egg yolk into each. Mask each yolk with the cream and sprinkle all over with the grated cheese.

Cook in the oven until just set and serve immediately.

Cèpes Au Gratin *Mushrooms Baked in Cream Sauce*

DAUPHINE

This area has a wealth of mushrooms – cèpes, morilles and chanterelles. Even using cultivated mushrooms, this simple dish makes a delicious appetizer.

Preparation time: 20 minutes
Cooking time: 20 minutes
To serve: 4

5 tablespoons butter
1 large onion, finely chopped
1 garlic clove, finely chopped
1½ lb mushrooms, thinly sliced
salt
freshly ground black pepper
1¼ cups crème fraîche (see page 118)
1 tablespoon fine dry white bread crumbs
1 tablespoon grated cheese

Melt ¼ cup of the butter in a heavy saucepan, add the onion and garlic and fry gently until softened. Add the mushrooms, cover and cook until they soften. Season to taste with salt and pepper.

Bring the crème fraîche to a boil in another saucepan. Add the juice drained off the mushroom mixture, stir well and boil gently until the cream thickens. Fold in the mushrooms.

Divide the mixture between buttered ramekin dishes, sprinkle with the bread crumbs and cheese and dot with the remaining butter. Brown quickly under a preheated broiler and serve.

Flamiche Aux Poireaux *Leek Tart*

PICARDY

This creamy leek tart appears in different guises in various parts of Northern France, sometimes with diced cooked ham added to the filling, sometimes with a pastry lid, so that it becomes more of a pie than a tart. This is the "pure" version as it is made in Picardy.

Preparation time: 30 minutes
Cooking time: 50 minutes
Oven temperature: 400°
To serve: 6

$\frac{1}{2}$ quantity pâte brisée (see page 114)
$\frac{1}{2}$ cup butter
3 lb leeks, white parts only, sliced
2 tablespoons flour
1$\frac{1}{4}$ cups milk
pinch of grated nutmeg
salt
freshly ground black pepper
2 eggs
$\frac{3}{4}$ cup heavy cream
1 cup shredded cheese

Roll out the dough and use to line a 10 inch tart or quiche pan. Prick the dough and bake blind for 10 minutes.

Melt half the butter in a heavy saucepan, add the leeks, cover and cook very gently, without allowing to color, for 10 minutes. Add just enough water to stop the leeks from burning and cook until tender.

In another saucepan melt 2 tablespoons of the butter, stir in the flour and cook for 3 minutes without allowing to brown. Gradually stir in the milk and the cooking liquid from the leeks until smooth. Bring briefly to a boil, add the nutmeg and salt and pepper to taste and simmer the sauce for a few minutes, stirring well.

Spread the leeks evenly in the pastry shell.

Beat the eggs with the cream and add to the cream sauce, together with half the grated cheese. Pour over the leeks. Sprinkle with the remaining cheese and dot with the remaining butter. Bake for 25 to 30 minutes or until the top is slightly risen and golden brown. Serve very hot.

Salade Chaude A La Flamande *Salad with Hot Dressing*

FLANDERS

This creamy salad dressing gives rather more body than usual to lettuce.

Preparation time: 10 minutes
Cooking time: 3 to 4 minutes
To serve: 4 to 6

2 heads of lettuce, leaves separated
4 eggs
2 tablespoons wine vinegar
salt
freshly ground black pepper
2 tablespoons butter

Arrange the lettuce leaves in a salad bowl.

Break the eggs into a bowl, add the vinegar and salt and pepper to taste and beat together with a fork.

Melt the butter in a heavy saucepan, add the egg mixture and stir over a gentle heat until the eggs just begin to thicken. Pour quickly over the lettuce, toss well and serve.

Feuilletés de Roquefort and pâté feuilletée (page 115)

Salade De Pissenlits Au Lard *Dandelion Salad with Bacon*

FLANDERS

Use young dandelion leaves, or, if your lawn does not grow enough of them, use one of the rather bitter salad greens such as chicory, for this traditional country salad.

Preparation time: 10 minutes
Cooking time: 5 minutes
To serve: 4

1 head of chicory or enough dandelion leaves
¼ lb bacon, finely diced
2 tablespoons wine vinegar
salt
freshly ground black pepper

Put the chicory or dandelion leaves in a salad bowl.

Quickly fry the diced bacon in a skillet until their fat has run and they are just beginning to crisp. Pour the contents of the skillet, fat and all, over the salad. Add the vinegar to the pan, let it bubble up and pour over the salad also. Add salt and pepper to taste and turn well. Serve quickly.

Feuilletés De Roquefort *Roquefort Puffs*

LANGUEDOC

Made with the wonderful sheep's milk cheese that has to be matured in the particular caves of Roquefort in order to earn its name, these are delicious appetizers, or *bonnes bouchés* to accompany an aperitif.

Preparation time: 15 minutes (plus pastry)
Cooking time: 15 to 20 minutes
Oven temperature: 425°
To serve: 6

$\frac{2}{3}$ *quantity pâte feuilletée (see page 115) or*
   puff pastry
$\frac{1}{2}$ *lb Roquefort cheese*
1 tablespoon brandy
2 tablespoons heavy cream
$\frac{1}{2}$ *cup finely chopped walnuts (optional)*
1 small egg
1 tablespoon water

Roll out the dough $\frac{1}{8}$ inch thick. Cut into 3 inch squares.

Crumble the cheese and blend it gently with the brandy, cream and walnuts, if used. There is no need to form a smooth paste.

Put a spoonful of the cheese mixture into the center of each dough square. Moisten the edges and fold over into a triangle. Seal the edges well and crimp them together. Place the triangles on a baking sheet. Brush with the egg lightly beaten with the water and bake in the oven until puffed up and golden brown. Serve hot.

Salade Aux Noix *Salad with Walnuts*

PITOU

Walnut oil has a wonderful deep flavor, but, like the nuts themselves, must be used fresh or it becomes musty. Use the new season's oil, and always keep it in the refrigerator.

Preparation time: 15 minutes
To serve: 4 to 6

1 garlic clove, halved
1 head of lettuce
$\frac{1}{4}$ *cup walnut oil*
1 slice of stale white bread, finely diced
$\frac{1}{2}$ *cup finely chopped walnuts*
1 tablespoon wine vinegar
pinch of sugar
salt
freshly ground black pepper

Rub the inside of a salad bowl hard with the cut surface of the garlic clove. Tear the lettuce leaves into convenient pieces and put into the bowl.

Heat 1 tablespoon of the oil in a skillet and quickly fry the diced bread, stirring well so that it browns on all sides. Scatter the bread croûtons over the lettuce leaves, together with the chopped walnuts.

Stir together the vinegar, sugar and salt and pepper to taste and slowly stir in the remaining walnut oil until the mixture is combined. Pour over the salad just before serving and toss well.

Les Artichauts A La Barigoule *Braised Artichokes*

PROVENCE

Use the small artichokes with pointed, purple-flushed leaves for this dish. They must be very young and fresh, so that they have not yet developed a hairy "choke." Serve as a hot hors d'oeuvre, allowing one or two artichokes per person.

Preparation time: 15 minutes
Cooking time: 15 to 20 minutes
To serve: 6

6 or 12 very young globe artichokes
¾ cup olive oil
¾ cup water
salt, preferably sea salt

Cut the stalks off the artichokes very close to the base, pull off the first layer of leaves and cut the remaining leaves down with kitchen scissors to within 1 inch of the base, or to where the leaves begin to be fleshy.

Put the artichokes side by side in a heavy, wide-bottomed saucepan, add the oil and water and bring quickly to a boil. Boil, uncovered, until almost all the liquid has evaporated. The artichokes should have crisp brown outer leaves, and be quite tender inside, and it should be possible to eat them whole.

Place on individual plates, sprinkle with the remaining cooking liquid and a little salt and serve.

Caviar Provençal *Eggplant Dip*

PROVENCE

Nothing could be more satisfying than a bowl of this "caviar," served with crusty French bread and a bottle of wine, for a light lunch, or to start a more substantial meal. The mixture can also be used for stuffing hard-cooked eggs, or served with raw vegetables (*crudités*), to make a more elaborate hors d'oeuvre.

Preparation time: about 45 minutes
Cooking time: 45 minutes to 1 hour
Oven temperature: 375°
To serve: 6

2 lb eggplants
3 garlic cloves, crushed
¼ cup olive oil
juice of ½ lemon
salt
freshly ground black pepper
chopped fresh parsley or 1 anchovy fillet to
    garnish

Slice the eggplants in half lengthwise and either broil very gently on both sides until very soft, or bake in the oven. This may take up to 1 hour, and you must be careful not to let the skin burn. Scoop out the flesh and place in a blender or mortar, together with the garlic. Blend together, then slowly add the oil, drop by drop, as for making mayonnaise. Add the lemon juice and season to taste with salt and pepper.

Serve in a bowl, garnished with parsley or a rolled anchovy fillet.

Salade De Champignons A La Crème _Raw Mushroom Salad_

ORLEANNAIS

Creamy mushroom salad in thick brown bowls can be bought by weight in _charcuteries_ and _alimentations_ and sometimes even at market stalls. It should be made with the brown-tinged champignons de Paris or with field mushrooms, but cultivated button mushrooms will also do. Moutarde de Meaux, the lovely grainy mustard made in the town of Meaux, not far from Paris, should ideally be used. Serve alone or as part of a mixed hors d'oeuvre.

Preparation time: 10 minutes
To serve: 4

½ lb button mushrooms, trimmed
lemon juice
2 teaspoons Moutarde de Meaux or Dijon-style mustard
¾ cup crème fraîche (see page 118) or heavy cream
salt
freshly ground black pepper
1 tablespoon finely chopped fresh parsley

Sprinkle the mushrooms with a little lemon juice.

Stir the mustard into the cream and season it generously with salt and pepper. If you are using heavy cream, add some extra lemon juice.

Fold the mushrooms into the cream, pile into a dark glazed bowl and sprinkle with the parsley before serving.

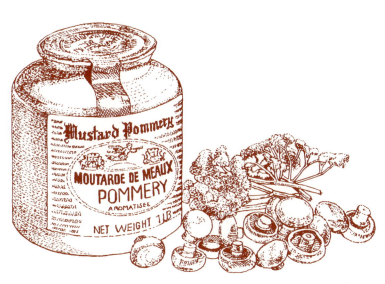

Salade Bourguignonne _Salad with Chicken Livers_

BURGUNDY

Chicken livers are to Bresse what goose liver is to the Alsace and the Perigord, and they are used in countless unexpected ways. This is a most unusual salad, which can be served on its own as an appetizer.

Preparation time: 10 minutes
Cooking time: 3 minutes
To serve: 4

¼ cup butter
¼ lb chicken livers, roughly chopped
1 teaspoon Dijon-style mustard
1 tablespoon wine vinegar
1 egg yolk
3 tablespoons oil
salt
freshly ground black pepper
1 head of lettuce

Melt the butter in a skillet, add the chicken livers and fry for 3 minutes – they should be just pink and set. Remove from the heat and chop finely.

Put the mustard into a bowl and stir in the vinegar. Add the egg yolk and stir until smooth. Dribble in the oil, stirring all the time to combine. Season to taste with salt and pepper and stir in the chicken livers.

Arrange the lettuce leaves in a salad bowl, pour over the chicken liver dressing and serve.

Terrine De Porc Pork Terrine

GASCOGNE

A robust coarse-textured country pâté, this is traditionally made when a pig has been killed on the farm. It makes an excellent mainstay for a summer lunch or buffet, served thickly sliced from an earthenware terrine.

Preparation time: 20 minutes (plus setting)
Cooking time: 1½ to 1¾ hours
Oven temperature: 425°; reduced to 375°
To serve: 8 to 12

2 to 2¼ lb fresh pork sides, skinned and
  boned
½ lb pork liver
1 onion, finely chopped
2 garlic cloves, finely chopped
2 fresh rosemary branches
1 egg
2 tablespoons brandy
salt
freshly ground black pepper
1 pig's foot, split in half
2 bay leaves

Grind the pork coarsely with the liver. Mix in the onion and garlic and the finely chopped leaves of one of the rosemary branches.

Beat the egg with the brandy and season well with salt and pepper. Mix into the meat. Fry a small pat of the mixture to taste for seasoning. Press the mixture evenly into a 1 quart terrine.

Blanch the pig's foot in boiling water for 2 minutes, then drain and press into the top of the terrine, together with the second branch of rosemary and the bay leaves. Place the terrine in a roasting pan, add cold water to the pan to come halfway up the terrine and place in the oven. Reduce the heat after 15 minutes, and continue to cook until the meat has shrunk away from the sides of the dish and the cooking juices are clear.

Remove the pig's foot, smooth the top and rearrange the rosemary and bay leaves. Leave to cool slightly, then weight down the pâté and leave for at least 1 day before serving, to allow it to set firmly and for the flavor to mature.

Pâté De Foie De Volaille Poultry Liver Pâté

ALSACE

Strasbourg is the home of foie gras, the grossly enlarged liver of geese that have been force-fed, and from which an amazingly rich pâté is made, sometimes enriched further still by the truffles of the Perigord district. That is a dish best left to the professionals, but a rich smooth pâté made of chicken livers or of a mixture of chicken and duck, and even on occasion a goose liver, is a treat that is very easy for the home cook to make.

Preparation time: 10 minutes (plus setting)
Cooking time: 7 minutes
To serve: 10 to 12

½ lb (1 cup) butter
1 lb poultry livers (see above)
2 tablespoons brandy
2 tablespoons Madeira
2 garlic cloves
¼ teaspoon dried mixed herbs
salt
freshly ground black pepper
1 bay leaf

Melt half the butter in a heavy skillet, add the livers and cook them over a moderate heat for 5 minutes, stirring so that they cook evenly. The livers should be brown on the outside, and pink, but set, in the center.

Pour the contents of the skillet into a blender or food processor. Pour the brandy and Madeira into the skillet and bring quickly to a boil, stirring well to incorporate any sediment left on the bottom of the pan. Allow to bubble for 1 minute, then add to the livers. Add the garlic and dried herbs and blend until smooth. Blend in the remaining butter and salt and pepper to taste.

Pour into one or several earthenware terrines, place a bay leaf on top and refrigerate overnight before serving.

If the pâté is to be kept for several days before serving, pour enough cooled, melted butter over the top to form a complete seal. The pâté will then keep for at least a week in the refrigerator.

Foie De Volaille Aux Raisins *Poultry Livers with Grapes*

GUYENNE

This southwest corner of France is famous above all for its fatted geese and their foie gras, sometimes weighing as much as 2 lb each. These are not only made into the world-renowned truffled pâté but are also sometimes served quite simply fried in butter. So are the livers of ducks and turkeys which are also raised a great deal here. Combined with the local chasselas grapes, they make a simple but rich and delicious first course or light dish. Use the liver of whichever bird you are cooking, and supplement with chicken livers if necessary.

Preparation time: 10 minutes
Cooking time: 10 minutes
To serve: 4 to 6

1 lb poultry livers (see above)
6 oz ($\frac{3}{4}$ cup) butter
4 to 6 slices of white bread
salt
freshly ground black pepper
$\frac{3}{4}$ cup white wine or dry vermouth
$\frac{1}{2}$ lb seedless green grapes, peeled

Pick over the livers and cut the larger livers of geese, turkeys or ducks into thick slices. Leave chicken livers whole.

Melt $\frac{1}{4}$ cup of the butter in a heavy skillet and quickly brown the slices of bread on both sides. Set aside and keep warm on a heated serving plate.

Add the remaining butter to the clean skillet and when it begins to foam put in the livers, spreading them out so that they can cook evenly. Cook for 3 minutes on each side, but no more – they should be brown on the outside and pink but set inside. Season generously with salt and pepper and divide between the pieces of fried bread. Keep hot.

Add the wine or vermouth to the skillet, stir well to loosen any sediment and bring quickly to a boil. Boil for 1 minute to reduce. Add the grapes to the pan and allow to heat through, then pour over the livers. Serve hot.

Terrine de porc and foie de volaille aux raisins

Quiche Lorraine *Bacon and Egg Quiche*

LORRAINE

This well-known specialty should be just creamily set and delicately flavored with the smoked ham of the region. Failing this, smoked pork or bacon may also be used.

Preparation time: 15 minutes (plus pastry)
Cooking time: 45 to 50 minutes
Oven temperature: 375°
To serve: 4 to 6

½ quantity pâte brisée (see page 114)
¼ lb smoked ham, pork or bacon, cubed
3 eggs
1¼ cups crème fraîche (see page 118) or
   heavy cream
salt
freshly ground black pepper

Roll out the dough and use to line a 9 inch tart or quiche pan, preferably one with a removable base. Prick the dough all over with a fork and bake blind for 10 minutes.

Meanwhile, fry the ham, pork or bacon lightly in a skillet to let some of the fat run. Drain on paper towels.

Beat the eggs in a bowl together with the cream. Season to taste with salt and pepper. Scatter the pieces of ham, pork or bacon evenly over the bottom of the pastry shell. Pour in the egg and cream mixture and return to the oven. Bake for a further 35 to 40 minutes or until the eggs have just set and the top of the filling is golden. Check the quiche from time to time and prick any bubbles that may form. Serve hot or cold.

Quiche Aux Oignons *Alsatian Onion Quiche*

ALSACE

This creamy quiche has a strong onion flavor.

Preparation time: 30 minutes (plus pastry)
Cooking time: 30 minutes
Oven temperature: 425°
To serve: 6

½ quantity pâte brisée (see page 114)
¼ cup lard
1 lb onions, thinly sliced
¼ lb smoked pork or bacon, diced
salt
freshly ground black pepper
2 tablespoons butter
¼ cup flour
1½ cups milk
1 egg yolk
1 tablespoon crème fraîche (see page 118)
   or heavy cream
⅛ teaspoon grated nutmeg

Roll out the dough and use to line a 9 inch tart or quiche pan, preferably one with a removable base. Prick the dough all over with a fork and bake blind for 10 minutes.

Melt the lard in a skillet and add the onions. Cook them over a moderately high heat until they are just golden brown. If you are using bacon, fry it together with the onions and use a little less lard. Season to taste with salt and pepper. Remove from the heat.

Melt the butter in a saucepan, stir in the flour and cook over a gentle heat for 3 minutes without allowing to brown. Add the milk and stir until you have a smooth sauce. Bring to a boil, then lower the heat and simmer, stirring, until the sauce thickens.

Distribute the onions and the smoked pork or bacon evenly over the bottom of the pastry shell. Mix the egg yolk with the cream and add to the sauce. Season to taste with salt and pepper and add the nutmeg. Pour the sauce evenly into the pastry shell and return to the oven. Bake for a further 20 minutes or until the filling is set. Serve very hot.

Fish and
Shellfish

Homard Grillé *Broiled Lobster in Cream Sauce*

BRITANNY

Homard à l'Amoricaine, as the Bretons insist that it should really be called after the ancient name of the kingdom of Brittany, is one of the classic restaurant dishes that are perhaps more hallowed by reputation than by eating. This is a simplified version, which is nonetheless rich and wonderful for a special occasion. A similar dish is also made with crayfish that are caught off the Breton coast.

Preparation time: 30 minutes
Cooking time: 30 minutes
To serve: 2 to 3

1 lobster, freshly cooked
½ lb tomatoes, peeled and roughly chopped
2 tablespoons finely chopped shallots
¾ cup white wine
1 cup heavy cream
2 tablespoons flour
1 tablespoon butter
1 teaspoon Dijon-style mustard
salt
freshly ground black pepper
2 tablespoons brandy
1 tablespoon grated Parmesan, Gruyère or
   Cheddar cheese

Extract the lobster meat from the shell, discarding the gray sac in the head and the intestinal canal that runs through the body and tail. Arrange the meat in a gratin dish and keep warm.

Put the tomatoes, shallots and white wine in a saucepan, bring to a boil and simmer until reduced to a soft purée.

Bring the cream to a boil in another saucepan and simmer until it begins to thicken.

Make a beurre manié by working the flour into the butter. Add this to the cream and stir until smooth. Pass the tomato mixture through a fine sieve and add the purée to the cream. Add the mustard and salt and pepper to taste. Bring quickly to almost boiling point.

Warm the brandy, set alight and pour over the lobster. Pour on the sauce, which should completely cover the lobster, smooth the top and sprinkle with the cheese. Heat through and brown quickly under a preheated broiler before serving.

Moules A La Marinière *Mussels Cooked in White Wine*

BRITTANY

The most classic of all the mussel dishes, this is usually served from a big tureen. Everyone helps themselves into deep soup plates, and a few extra plates are left on the table for the discarded mussel shells. Experienced mussel eaters use an empty double shell in a pincer action to eat each mussel, and an empty single shell to scoop up the delicious liquid. All else that is needed is chunks of French bread for mopping up, and a few finger bowls.

Preparation time: 20 minutes (plus cleaning mussels)
Cooking time: 6 minutes
To serve: 6 to 8

1 bottle of white wine
2 onions, finely chopped
1 bouquet garni
3 quarts fresh mussels, cleaned
2 tablespoons finely chopped fresh parsley

Put the wine in a very large saucepan together with the onions and the bouquet garni and bring to a boil. Boil rapidly for about 3 minutes in order to evaporate the liquid a little.

Add the mussels, cover the pan and cook over a high heat until the mussels open. Shake the pan occasionally so that the mussels will change position and cook evenly. If the pan is too heavy to shake effectively, use a slotted spoon to move the mussels around.

Discard any mussels that remain closed after 6 minutes and pour the remainder into the heated tureen. Sprinkle with the parsley and serve very hot.

Crabe Gratinée A La Bretonne *Crab in Cream Sauce*

BRITTANY

A very rich and filling but quite inexpensive dish, this can be served as an appetizer or main course. Spider crabs may also be used.

Preparation time: 30 minutes
Cooking time: 20 minutes
To serve: 4 to 6

2 large crabs, cooked
½ cup butter
½ cup flour
¾ cup white wine
2½ cups milk
2 tablespoons crème fraîche (see page 118)
  or heavy cream
1 egg yolk
salt
freshly ground black pepper
1 tablespoon fine dry white bread crumbs

Extract all the meat from the crabs and set aside. Scrub the body shells and reserve.

Melt 6 tablespoons of the butter in a large saucepan. Stir in the flour and cook, without allowing to brown, for 3 minutes. Add the wine and stir to a smooth paste. Slowly stir in the milk until smooth and simmer for 5 minutes.

Mix the crème fraîche with the egg yolk and add to the pan with salt and pepper to taste. Stir in the crab meat. Spoon the mixture into the crab shells; pour any that is left over into a shallow gratin dish. Sprinkle with the bread crumbs, dot with the remaining butter and brown quickly under a preheated broiler.

Crabe gratinée a la Bretonne,
homard grillé and moules à la marinière

Mouclade *Mussels in Cream Sauce*

BRITTANY

This is a richer and more elegant dish than Moules à la Marinière, suitable for formal occasions. In a restaurant the mussels would probably be served each in their half shell, but for cooking at home it is simpler to serve them in a gratin dish without the shells.

Preparation time: 20 minutes (plus cleaning mussels)
Cooking time: 15 minutes
To serve: 6 as a main dish, or 10 as an appetizer

2 cups white wine
1 onion, finely chopped
1 garlic clove, finely chopped
1 bouquet garni (bay leaf and parsley and fennel sprigs)
$\frac{1}{2}$ teaspoon curry powder
3 quarts fresh mussels, cleaned
5 tablespoons butter
$\frac{1}{4}$ cup flour
$\frac{3}{4}$ cup crème fraîche (see page 118)
2 egg yolks
large squeeze of lemon juice
salt
freshly ground black pepper
1 tablespoon finely chopped fresh parsley

Put the wine in a wide saucepan together with the onion, garlic, bouquet garni and curry powder, and bring to a boil. Add the mussels, cover the pan and cook over a high heat until the mussels open. Shake the pan occasionally so that the mussels will change position and cook evenly. If the pan is too heavy to shake effectively, use a slotted spoon to move the mussels around.

Remove the mussels with a slotted spoon as they open and discard any that remain closed after 6 minutes. Discard the shells and arrange the mussels in a heated gratin dish. Keep warm.

Boil the cooking liquid rapidly for a few minutes to reduce. Strain and reserve 2 cups. In a clean pan melt $\frac{1}{4}$ cup of the butter, add the flour and cook gently, without allowing to brown, for 3 minutes. Slowly stir in the reserved cooking liquid until smooth, then bring to a boil and simmer for 1 to 2 minutes or until the sauce thickens.

Mix the crème fraîche with the egg yolks and lemon juice. Stir in a little of the hot sauce, then add to the remaining sauce in the pan. Stir in salt and pepper to taste. Add the remaining butter, cut into very small pieces, to give the sauce a glaze; pour it over the mussels in the dish and sprinkle with the parsley before serving.

Truites A La Bretonne *Fried Trout with Potatoes and Capers*

BRITTANY

An "all in one" dish, this tastes every bit as good as it looks.

Preparation time: 15 minutes
Cooking time: 25 minutes
To serve: 4

4 trout, dressed
2 tablespoons flour
salt
freshly ground black pepper
½ cup butter
2 tablespoons oil
1 lb potatoes, peeled and diced
¼ lb cooked shrimp, shelled and deveined
2 tablespoons roughly chopped capers
1 tablespoon finely chopped fresh parsley

Dry the trout on paper towels, then dredge them in the well-seasoned flour. Brush excess flour off so that they have just a thin even covering.

Melt half the butter with 1 tablespoon of the oil in a heavy skillet. Add the potatoes and cook over a moderate heat until tender and beginning to brown, turning from time to time.

Meanwhile, melt the remaining butter with the remaining oil in another large heavy skillet. When sizzling hot, put in the trout. Cook for 8 to 10 minutes on each side – they should be cooked and golden brown, with a crisp skin.

Add the shrimp and the capers to the potatoes. Heat through, then add salt and pepper to taste.

Arrange the trout on a heated serving dish, scatter the potato, shrimp and caper mixture over and around the trout and sprinkle with the parsley. Serve very hot.

Filets De Sole Deauville *Fillets of Sole with Onion Sauce*

NORMANDY

Onion and sole blend remarkably well in this dish, which combines so many of Normandy's favorite products.

Preparation time: 15 minutes
Cooking time: 30 minutes
To serve: 4

3 to 4 sole, filleted and bones reserved
1 small onion, quartered
¾ cup cider
1 lemon slice
1 bay leaf
1 parsley sprig
5 tablespoons butter
½ lb onions, finely chopped
¾ cup crème fraîche (see page 118)
pinch of grated nutmeg
½ teaspoon Dijon-style mustard
squeeze of lemon juice
salt
freshly ground black pepper
2 tablespoons fine dry white bread crumbs

Put the fish bones in a large saucepan, add the quartered onion, cider, lemon slice, bay leaf and parsley and cover with cold water. Bring to a boil and boil briskly for 10 minutes. Strain the stock.

Melt ¼ cup of the butter in a heavy saucepan, add the chopped onions and cook very gently until they are quite soft and almost puréed, but barely colored.

Meanwhile poach the fish fillets in the fish stock for 5 minutes. Lift them out gently and place in a buttered gratin dish. Keep warm. Reserve the stock.

Add ¼ cup of the fish stock to the onions, then stir in the crème fraîche, nutmeg, mustard, lemon juice and salt and pepper to taste. Pour the sauce over the sole, sprinkle on the bread crumbs and dot with the remaining butter. Brown quickly under a preheated broiler before serving.

Coquilles St Jacques A La Dieppoise

Scallops with Shrimp and Mussels
NORMANDY

These are most attractive when served in the deeper top shells of the scallops. If frozen scallops have to be used, the dish may be cooked in small ramekin dishes. One per person makes a delicious appetizer, two an ample main dish.

Preparation time: 15 minutes (plus cleaning mussels)
Cooking time: 30 minutes
To serve: 4 or 8 (see above)

$\frac{1}{2}$ pint fresh mussels, cleaned
$\frac{3}{4}$ cup white wine or cider
$\frac{3}{4}$ cup water
8 scallops, detached from their shells and cleaned
$\frac{1}{4}$ lb button mushrooms, quartered
1 onion, finely chopped
$\frac{1}{4}$ lb cooked shrimp, shelled and deveined
$\frac{1}{4}$ cup flour
$\frac{1}{4}$ cup butter
$\frac{1}{4}$ cup crème fraîche (see page 118) or heavy cream
salt
freshly ground black pepper
2 tablespoons fine dry white bread crumbs

Put the mussels in a large saucepan with half the wine or cider and half the water. Cover the pan and cook over a high heat until the mussels open. Remove the mussels with a slotted spoon as soon as they have opened, take the meat from the shells and set aside. Discard any mussels that remain closed. Strain the cooking liquid and reserve.

Put the scallops, mushrooms and onion in another saucepan, add the remaining wine or cider and water and poach for 6 to 8 minutes, until the scallops are opaque and tender. Remove from the heat. Take out the scallops with a slotted spoon and place one in each well-washed scallop shell. Surround with the poached mushrooms, shrimp and mussels.

Add the mussel liquid to the liquid left in the pan and boil briskly for 2 minutes to reduce, Strain and return to the pan.

Make a beurre manié by working the flour into half the butter. Add to the pan and simmer, stirring, for 2 minutes. Stir in the crème fraîche and salt and pepper to taste. Pour the sauce gently over the scallops in the shells, sprinkle with the bread crumbs and dot with the remaining butter. Heat through and brown under a preheated broiler.

Harengs A La Dieppoise

NORMANDY

Made in this harbor town, with herrings fresh from the sea, this is a delicious hors d'oeuvre.

Preparation time: 10 minutes (plus cooling)
Cooking time: 15 to 20 minutes
To serve: 6

$1\frac{1}{4}$ cups white wine or cider
$\frac{3}{4}$ cup wine vinegar
$\frac{3}{4}$ cup water
1 carrot, thinly sliced
2 onions, cut into rings
1 bouquet garni
12 peppercorns, lightly crushed
6 fresh herrings, dressed
1 lemon, sliced

Coquilles Gratinées St Michel

Scallops with Cheese and Cream

NORMANDY

A very simple way of cooking scallops, this is nonetheless very rich. Serve in the deep top scallop shell if possible. One per person makes a delicious first course, two a good main dish.

Preparation time: 15 minutes
Cooking time: 30 minutes
To serve: 4 or 8 (see above)

8 sea scallops, detached from their shells
    and cleaned
1 onion, finely chopped
$\frac{3}{4}$ cup white wine or cider
$\frac{3}{4}$ cup water
$\frac{1}{4}$ cup flour
5 tablespoons butter
2 tablespoons grated Gruyère, Parmesan or
    Cheddar cheese
$\frac{1}{4}$ cup crème fraîche (see page 118) or
    heavy cream
salt
freshly ground black pepper
2 tablespoons fine dry white bread crumbs

Put the scallops into a saucepan with the onion, wine or cider and water and poach for 6 to 8 minutes or until the scallops are opaque and tender. Remove the scallops from the pan with a slotted spoon, slice thickly and set aside.

Boil the cooking liquid briskly for 2 minutes to reduce, then strain and return to the pan. Make a beurre manié by working the flour into $\frac{1}{4}$ cup of the butter. Add to the pan and simmer, stirring, for 2 minutes. Stir in half the cheese, the crème fraîche and salt and pepper to taste.

Return the scallops to the sauce and heat through, then pour into the scallop shells. Sprinkle with the bread crumbs mixed with the remaining cheese, dot with the remaining butter and brown quickly under a preheated broiler.

Put the wine or cider in a wide saucepan with the vinegar, water, carrot, 1 onion, the bouquet garni and peppercorns. Bring to a boil and boil briskly for 5 minutes.

Lower the heat and put the herrings into the pan. Poach very gently for 10 to 12 minutes or until cooked. The herrings must not be allowed to disintegrate. Remove from the heat.

Leave the herrings to cool in the marinade, preferably overnight. Lift out with a slotted spatula and arrange on a shallow serving dish. Strain over the marinade. Garnish with the second onion and the lemon slices.

Coquilles gratinées St Michel,
harengs à la Dieppoise and
coquilles St Jacques à la Dieppoise

Sole Dieppoise *Fillets of Sole with Mussels*

NORMANDY

Ancestor of the restaurant favorite, "sole normande," which was in fact invented by a Parisian restaurateur (perhaps even the great Carême?), this is a simpler country version.

Preparation time: 15 minutes (plus cleaning mussels)
Cooking time: 30 minutes
Oven temperature: 350°
To serve: 4

4 sole, dressed and skinned
salt
freshly ground black pepper
2 cups white wine or cider
1 quart fresh mussels, cleaned
1 onion, finely chopped
2 parsley sprigs
3 tablespoons butter
¼ cup flour
½ lb cooked shrimp, shelled and deveined
   (optional)
squeeze of lemon juice

Season the sole well with salt and pepper on both sides and lay in a shallow, enameled or porcelain, baking dish. Pour on half the white wine or cider, cover with cooking parchment paper and foil and cook in the oven for 10 to 15 minutes, according to size.

Meanwhile put the mussels in a large saucepan with the remaining wine or cider, half the chopped onion and the parsley. Cover the pan and cook over a high heat until the mussels open. Remove the mussels with a slotted spoon as soon as they open, take the meat from the shells and keep warm. Discard any mussels that remain closed. Strain the cooking liquid and reserve.

In another saucepan, melt 2 tablespoons of the butter, add the remaining onion and cook over a gentle heat until soft. Sprinkle on the flour and cook, stirring and not allowing to brown, for 3 minutes. Slowly add the strained mussel cooking liquid.

When the sole is cooked, remove it from the oven and pour off the liquid into another saucepan. Boil briskly until reduced almost to a glaze. Add to the sauce.

Arrange the mussels and shrimp, if used, around the sole in the baking dish. Add the lemon juice to the sauce and adjust the seasoning. Add the remaining butter, cut into small pieces, to give the sauce a glaze. Pour over the fish, return to the oven for a few minutes to reheat and serve.

Saumon A L'Oseille *Salmon with Sorrel Sauce*

NIVERNAIS

Salmon are often served in the Loire area, sometimes, as here, with a green purée of sorrel – a feast for the eyes as well as the palate. Salmon steaks may be cooked in the same way, with the steaks laid on a bed of sorrel purée.

Preparation time: 30 minutes
Cooking time: about 20 minutes
Oven temperature: 350°
To serve: 4 to 6

¼ cup butter
1 tablespoon finely chopped shallots
1 lb sorrel leaves, stripped of the thicker
   stalks
dash of dry vermouth
salt
freshly ground black pepper
pinch of grated nutmeg
¾ cup crème fraîche (see page 118)
1 salmon, drawn and scaled
¾ cup dry white wine

Melt the butter in a heavy saucepan, add the shallots and fry until softened. Add the sorrel leaves and the vermouth, cover the pan and cook for a few minutes until the sorrel has wilted and is almost puréed. Add salt and pepper to taste and the nutmeg and stir in half the cream.

Stuff the salmon with this mixture, and lay it in a buttered shallow baking dish. Pour on the wine, cover with a sheet of buttered cooking parchment paper and then foil and cook in the oven until done. The time taken will vary with the size of the fish; you should lift the foil and test after 20 minutes, as the fish should not be allowed to overcook.

When ready, pour off the cooking liquid into a small saucepan, add the remaining cream and bring quickly to a boil. Boil for 1 to 2 minutes to reduce. Adjust the seasoning, then pour gently around the fish and serve.

Matelote De Maqueraux *Mackerel Stewed in Wine*

ARTOIS

A sturdy fisherman's stew, this is made in Artois with the mackerel that are caught in great abundance in the short stretch of water that divides England from France around Calais and Boulogne. In other parts of France it may be made with eel – not so dissimilar from mackerel in their rich meatiness. Further south, in Burgundy, a similar dish will be made using red wine.

Preparation time: 20 minutes
Cooking time: 30 minutes
To serve: 6

6 tablespoons butter
1 large onion, sliced
1 large carrot, sliced
1 garlic clove, finely chopped
3 large mackerel, dressed and cut into
*   2 inch slices*
1¼ cups dry white wine
1 bouquet garni (bay leaf, parsley and
*   fennel)*
salt
freshly ground black pepper
½ lb button mushrooms

Melt ¼ cup of the butter in a heavy saucepan, add the vegetables and cook gently until soft. Do not allow them to brown.

Lay the pieces of mackerel on top of the bed of vegetables, add the wine, bouquet garni and salt and pepper to taste and bring to a boil. Cover and simmer for 15 to 20 minutes or until the fish is just done, but has not begun to disintegrate.

While the fish is cooking, melt the remaining butter in a skillet, add the mushrooms and fry quickly over a high heat.

Lift the fish out carefully with a slotted spoon and place in a heated tureen. Add some of the pieces of carrot and the onion slices. Scatter the mushrooms over the fish. Bring the remaining cooking liquid to a boil and boil fiercely for 2 minutes to reduce. Pour it over the fish and serve.

Truite Au Riesling *Trout Cooked in Riesling*

ALSACE

A perfect marriage of the fresh little trout from the mountain streams and the sparklingly crisp dry local wine, this dish is a specialty of the mountainous Vosges.

Preparation time: 15 minutes
Cooking time: 25 minutes
Oven temperature: 400°
To serve: 4

4 trout, dressed
salt
freshly ground black pepper
5 tablespoons butter
2 tablespoons finely chopped shallots
1 cup Riesling or dry white wine
1 cup thinly sliced mushrooms
¾ cup crème fraîche (see page 118) or
*   heavy cream*

Garnish
½ tablespoon finely chopped fresh parsley
4 lemon slices

Wipe the trout inside and out and season lightly with salt and pepper. Melt 2 tablespoons of the butter in a small saucepan, add the shallots and fry until softened. Spread the shallots on the bottom of a shallow baking dish, wide enough to hold the trout lying side by side. Lay the trout on top. Bring the wine quickly to a boil in the saucepan and pour over the trout in the dish. Cover with buttered cooking parchment paper and then with foil, place in the oven and cook for 10 to 15 minutes, according to the size of the trout.

Soften the mushrooms in 2 tablespoons of the butter and season lightly with salt and pepper.

When the fish is cooked, remove it from the oven and carefully pour off the cooking liquid. Strain this into a clean saucepan, bring to a boil and boil rapidly, uncovered, until it has reduced by about half.

Meanwhile take the skin very carefully off the trout, being careful not to let them break up. If they seem too delicate to turn over, take the skin off the top only.

When the cooking liquid has begun to thicken, pour in the juice from the mushrooms and stir in the cream. Adjust the seasoning and add the mushrooms and the remaining butter, cut into small pieces, to give the sauce a glaze. Pour the sauce carefully over the trout and garnish each fish with a parsley-sprinkled slice of lemon. Serve hot.

Cabillaud A La Flamande Cod à la Flamande

Cod is a fish which is often dried, salted and served in a stew in France. The fresh version is found mostly on the north-western sea coast where this delicious treatment originates.

Preparation time: 15 minutes
Cooking time: 15 minutes
Oven temperature: 350°
To serve: 4

2 lb fresh cod fillet, cut into 4 equal pieces
salt
freshly ground black pepper
$\frac{1}{4}$ cup butter
1 tablespoon chopped shallots
2 tablespoons chopped fresh parsley
$\frac{3}{4}$ cup dry white wine
4 lemon slices

Season the cod pieces with salt and pepper. Place the pieces side by side in a flameproof casserole, which has been rubbed generously with some of the butter and sprinkled with the shallots and a tablespoon of the parsley. Pour the wine over the fish. On each piece place a slice of lemon. Bring to a boil on top of the stove, then cover and place in the oven for about 12 minutes to finish cooking.

Remove the cod from the oven and drain, reserving the cooking liquid. Place the fish on a heated serving plate. Bring the liquid to a boil on top of the stove and boil to reduce by half. Stir in the remaining butter. Pour over the fish and sprinkle with the remaining parsley.

Poisson Grillé Au Fenouil Broiled Fish with Fennel

PROVENCE

Any very fresh, medium-sized fish, such as bass, porgy or mullet, is excellent prepared in this way, especially if cooked out of doors over charcoal to which a few branches of fennel have been added. But even cooked indoors, under the broiler, it is delicious, and the combination of the aniseed flavor of the fennel with the slightly charred skin and moist flesh of fresh fish is quite irresistible.

Preparation time: 10 minutes (plus making
   butter)
Cooking time: 15 to 25 minutes
To serve: 6

$6\frac{1}{2}$ lb fish (see above), allowing 1 small or
   $\frac{1}{2}$ larger fish per person, dressed
bunch of fresh fennel
salt
freshly ground black pepper
lemon juice
2 tablespoons olive oil
Montpellier butter (see page 111) to garnish

Cut deep diagonal slashes in the side of the fish, and insert a sprig of fennel in each. Place a sprig of fennel in the cavity of each fish also, together with a good sprinkling of salt and pepper. Rub the outside of each fish with salt and pepper and place them on the grid of the barbecue or wire rack of the broiler pan. If using a broiler pan, line it with foil to catch the juices.

Dribble some lemon juice and olive oil over each fish, put another sprig of fennel on top of each one and place under the preheated broiler or over the hot charcoal embers.

When one side of the fish is done, and its skin is lightly charred, turn over carefully. Sprinkle the other side with lemon juice and oil, place another branch of fennel on top and cook until this side is done also. Pour the cooking juices over the fish when serving, with Montpellier butter.

*Beurre de Montpellier (page 111), gigot de mer with ratatouille,
and poisson grillé au fenouil*

Gigot De Mer *Baked Fish*

PROVENCE

A whole sea bass, or a large piece of monkfish, is often spiked with garlic and baked in the oven, just like a leg of lamb – hence the name. It may be served with a salad, but is more often served in Provence with a ratatouille, as below.

Preparation time: 15 minutes (plus making
  ratatouille)
Cooking time: 30 to 40 minutes
Oven temperature: 375°
To serve: 6

$4\frac{1}{2}$ *to* $5\frac{1}{2}$ *lb whole fish or thick slice, dressed*
2 garlic cloves, cut into slivers
1 tablespoon olive oil
2 onions, thinly sliced
2 bay leaves
salt
freshly ground black pepper
1 fresh thyme sprig
2 fresh parsley sprigs
1 lemon, thinly sliced
$\frac{3}{4}$ *cup dry white wine or dry vermouth*
ratatouille (see page 105)

Cut diagonal slits all over the surface of the fish, and insert a sliver of garlic in each.

Line a baking dish with foil and oil the foil with about 1 teaspoon of the olive oil. Use half the sliced onion to make a bed for the fish, top with a bay leaf and lay the fish on top. Put salt, pepper, thyme and parsley inside the fish and cover with the remaining onion and bay leaf and half the lemon slices. Dribble on the remaining olive oil. Pour over the wine or vermouth and bake for 30 to 40 minutes, basting from time to time, until the fish is just cooked. Test by inserting a knife gently near the backbone – the flesh should come away fairly easily and be only the palest pink.

Spread the ratatouille in a shallow ovenproof serving dish.

Remove the fish carefully from the baking dish onto a plate. Discard the bay leaves and lemon slices, then pour the remaining contents of the baking dish over the ratatouille.

Fillet the fish carefully and lay it, skin side up, on top of the ratatouille. Return to the oven briefly to heat through, and serve garnished with the remaining lemon slices.

Truite Au Jambon Bayonne *Trout with Bayonne Ham*

BEARN

Bayonne, in the southwest corner of France, is the coastal outpost of French Basque cuisine. It is famous for its fish, peppers and, especially, its ham. Like Italian Parma and German Westphalian hams, it is usually smoked and aged, then sliced very thinly and served raw as a first course. In this recipe, its delicate smokey flavor is a perfect foil to the buttery, flaky trout flesh.

Preparation time: 25 minutes
Cooking time: 20 to 25 minutes
Oven temperature: 350°
To serve: 4

$\frac{1}{4}$ cup butter
2 tablespoons finely chopped shallots
4 medium-size trout, dressed but with heads still on
4 large pieces Bayonne ham (Parma ham may be used if more readily available)
$\frac{3}{4}$ cup dry white wine
chopped fresh parsley
watercress and thin slices of lemon (optional)

Melt the butter in a large flameproof casserole. Add the shallots and stir until golden. Remove the casserole from the heat.

Rinse the trout and pat dry. Wrap each trout in a large piece of the ham. Place the four fish in the casserole, and pour the white wine over. Return to the heat until the wine begins to simmer.

Cover the dish with a tight-fitting lid or, alternatively, a sheet of foil. Bake in the oven for 20 to 25 minutes or until the trout are just firm. Let the fish cool slightly, then carefully lift them from the casserole to a heated serving platter. Garnish with the parsley and serve.

This is also good cold as a luncheon dish or an elegant first course. If the fish is to be served cold, let it cool in the casserole. Before serving, gently unwrap the ham from each fish, and skin it. This is very easy once the fish is cooked; remove the skin in strips, beginning at the tail and pulling towards the head using a small sharp knife. When all the fish have been skinned, rewrap them in the ham, and serve garnished with watercress and thin slices of lemon.

Truites Bourguignonnes *Trout Cooked in Red Wine*

BURGUNDY

Although it may seem strange to cook trout in red wine, this is an excellent dish.

Preparation time: 15 minutes
Cooking time: 35 minutes
To serve: 6

1 bottle of red Burgundy wine
$\frac{3}{4}$ cup water
2 carrots, quartered
2 onions, quartered
1 bouquet garni (bay leaf and fennel, thyme and parsley sprigs)
salt
freshly ground black pepper
6 trout, dressed
2 tablespoons finely chopped shallots
$\frac{3}{4}$ cup butter, preferably unsalted
juice of 1 lemon
1 tablespoon finely chopped fresh parsley
1 lemon, sliced, to garnish

Make a court-bouillon by bringing the wine and water to a boil in a saucepan. Add the carrots, onions, bouquet garni and salt and pepper and boil steadily for 15 minutes. The liquid should be reduced by about half.

Rub the insides of the trout with salt and place them side by side in a shallow flameproof casserole or fish poacher. Strain on the boiling court-bouillon and poach the trout very gently for 10 to 15 minutes or until just cooked.

Pour or skim off $\frac{3}{4}$ cup of the court-bouillon and bring rapidly to a boil in a separate saucepan. Boil until reduced by half. Add the shallots and the butter, cut into small pieces, and stir until well combined. Add the lemon juice, adjust the seasoning and sprinkle with the parsley. Pour into a heated sauceboat and keep hot.

Lift the trout onto a heated serving dish, garnish with lemon slices and serve hot, with the sauce.

Poultry

Caneton Aux Navets

Duck with Turnips
MAINE

Duck is eaten so frequently in northern France that it is served in many different ways – sometimes, as in this recipe, braised and surrounded by local vegetables.

Preparation time: 20 minutes
Cooking time: 1¼ hours
Oven temperature: 375°
To serve: 4 to 6

1 large dressed duck
salt
freshly ground black pepper
¼ cup butter
¾ cup dry white wine
2 cups duck, chicken or veal broth
1 bouquet garni
1 lb baby turnips, peeled
1 lb pearl onions, peeled
1 teaspoon sugar
1 tablespoon flour

Wipe the duck well and prick the skin all over with a sharp-pronged fork. Rub salt and pepper into the skin and into the cavity.

Heat half the butter until foaming in a large flameproof casserole, add the duck and brown it all over. Pour off the fat into another flameproof casserole or heavy saucepan and set aside.

Add the wine to the duck in the first casserole, raise the heat and boil the wine to reduce. Add the broth, return to a boil and add the bouquet garni and salt and pepper to taste. Cover and place in the preheated oven, or cook over a low heat on top of the stove so that the liquid is barely simmering, for another 45 to 50 minutes.

Meanwhile, brown the turnips and onions in the butter in the second casserole. Sprinkle with the sugar, season generously, cover and leave to braise over a very low heat for 25 to 35 minutes or until tender.

When the duck is nearly cooked (test by pricking a drumstick with a sharp fork: the liquid which comes out should be just colorless) remove it from the casserole, cut it into serving pieces and keep warm on a deep serving platter. Make a beurre manié by blending the flour with the remaining butter. Add to the liquid in the casserole and stir until smooth. Bring to a boil and simmer for 2 minutes, stirring.

Surround the duck with drained braised vegetables and pour over the sauce just before serving.

Poulet A La Vallée D'Auge

NORMANDY

This dish can be found, with variations, all over Normandy. This version uses all the possible ingredients, but both the apples and the cider can be omitted – the essentials are the Calvados and the crème fraîche.

Preparation time: 20 minutes
Cooking time: about 50 minutes
To serve: 4 to 6

1 tablespoon flour
salt
freshly ground black pepper
1 roaster chicken, cut up, or 4 to 6 chicken
  pieces
½ cup butter
2 tart apples, peeled, cored and diced
¾ cup Calvados
¾ cup cider
¾ cup crème fraîche (see page 118)

Chicken with Cream and Apple Brandy

Season the flour generously with salt and pepper and roll the chicken pieces in it until they are well coated. Melt the butter in a flameproof casserole. When it is foaming, add the chicken pieces and cook them gently – they should only color to a pale gold. Add the apples and allow to soften.

Pour on the warmed Calvados and set it alight. When the flames have died down, stir in the cider. Cover and continue to simmer very gently until the chicken is cooked.

Stir in the crème fraîche, adjust the seasoning, bring just to a boil and serve.
Note: This is also an excellent way to cook pheasant, as it provides a lot of sauce for what can otherwise be a rather dry bird.

*Poulet à la Vallée d'Auge
and caneton à la bigarde*

Caneton A La Bigarde

Duck with Orange
NORMANDY

Ideally, this should be made with Seville oranges, as their rather bitter flavor adds an aromatic tang to the dish, counteracting the richness of the duck.

Preparation time: 20 minutes
Cooking time: 1½ hours
Oven temperature: 425°; reduced to 375°
To serve: 4 to 6

1 large dressed duck, with giblets
1 garlic clove, halved
salt
freshly ground black pepper
1 onion, chopped
1 carrot, chopped
1 bay leaf
finely pared rind and juice of 2 to 3 Seville
    oranges or 1 sweet navel orange
2 tablespoons butter
¼ cup flour
¾ cup dry white or red wine
pinch of sugar

Wipe the duck well and rub it, inside and out, with the cut surface of the clove of garlic. Discard the garlic. Rub salt liberally into the skin and prick it all over with a sharp-pronged fork. Put the duck on a rack in a roasting pan and roast for 15 minutes in the preheated oven, then lower the temperature and roast for a further 1¼ hours, or until the juice that runs out when you pierce the thickest part of the drumstick is clear or just pale pink. Pour off the fat from time to time.

Meanwhile, put the duck giblets, onion, carrot and bay leaf in a saucepan with plenty of water. Bring to a boil and simmer for 1 hour. Strain the stock and reserve 2 cups.

Cut the orange rind into very thin strips. (The rind of two of the Seville oranges is sufficient.) Plunge the strips into boiling water, boil for 3 minutes, then drain. Set aside.

Fifteen minutes before the duck is ready, begin to make the sauce. Melt the butter in a heavy saucepan, and allow to turn nutty brown. Add the flour, stir well and cook over a moderate heat until the mixture is pale caramel brown. Gradually stir in the wine, then add the strained giblet stock. Add the sugar and salt and pepper to taste and simmer over a moderate heat, stirring, until the sauce has thickened.

When the duck is ready, carve it into serving pieces and arrange them on a heated platter. Skim the fat from the juices that remain in the roasting pan and add to the sauce with the juice that has run from the duck when carving. Stir in the orange rind strips and juice. Heat through well and pour over the duck before serving.

Poulet Farci A La Cauchoise *Normandy Stuffed Chicken*

NORMANDY

This method of part braising, part roasting the bird produces a rich and juicy dish.

Preparation time: 30 minutes
Cooking time: 50 minutes to 1 hour
Oven temperature: 425°
To serve: 4 to 6

1 large roaster chicken, with giblets
6 tablespoons butter
2 onions, finely chopped
2 fresh tarragon branches, finely chopped, or
  1 teaspoon dried tarragon
6 oz (about ¾ cup) bulk sausage meat
1 thick slice of stale white bread
1 egg, lightly beaten
salt
freshly ground black pepper
2 tablespoons Calvados
1 lb pearl onions, peeled
2 cups cider
1 bouquet garni

Finely chop the chicken giblets, including the liver. Melt 2 tablespoons of the butter in a skillet, add the giblets, chopped onions and tarragon and fry gently, stirring well, until the onions are pale golden. Add the sausage meat and continue cooking, stirring, until all the mixture has changed color.

Meanwhile, soak the bread in water until softened. Squeeze out all excess moisture.

Turn the cooked sausage meat mixture into a bowl, add the squeezed out bread and the egg and mix well. Season to taste with salt and pepper and use to stuff the chicken. Rub the outside of the chicken with salt and pepper, then truss it.

Melt the remaining butter in a flameproof casserole. When foaming, add the chicken and fry until light golden brown all over. Pour on the warmed Calvados and set alight. When the flames die down, add the pearl onions and allow them to brown gently. Pour on the cider, add the bouquet garni and a little more salt and pepper and bring to a boil. Cover, lower the heat and simmer for 40 minutes.

Uncover the casserole, place in the oven and allow the top of the chicken to brown. Remove the chicken and onions to a heated serving dish. Discard the bouquet garni and boil the cooking liquid briskly to reduce before serving with the chicken.

Coq Au Vin Au Riesling *Chicken Cooked in Riesling Wine*

ALSACE

This classic Alsatian dish combines the local Riesling wine with the lovely yellow morel mushrooms that are one of the joys of the area, and eaten locally it has an incomparable flavor. A good dry white wine, and field or cultivated mushrooms, will still make a very excellent dish. Serve with noodles or simply a green salad.

Preparation time: 20 minutes
Cooking time: 1 hour 20 minutes
To serve: 4 to 6

1 roaster chicken, cut up, or 4 to 6 chicken
  pieces
salt
freshly ground black pepper
1 tablespoon flour
¼ cup butter
8 shallots, finely chopped
2 tablespoons brandy
1¼ cups Riesling or other white wine
½ lb morel or other mushrooms, sliced
¼ cup crème fraîche (see page 118) or
  heavy cream

Season the pieces of chicken and dust them very lightly with the flour. Melt the butter in a flameproof casserole and quickly brown the chicken pieces on all sides. Remove from the casserole and keep warm.

Add the shallots to the casserole and soften. Return the chicken pieces, pour on the brandy and set alight. When the flames have died down, add the wine and the mushrooms. Cover and simmer for about 1 hour, or until the chicken is cooked.

Remove the chicken pieces and arrange on a heated serving dish. Bring the cooking juices to a boil and boil briskly for a few minutes to reduce. Lower the heat. Add the cream and stir to make a smooth sauce. Adjust the seasoning. Pour the sauce carefully over the pieces of chicken to coat them and serve very hot.

56

Caneton Aux Cerises _Duck with Cherries_

ILE DE FRANCE

The Ile de France used to be known as the garden of Paris, and once the orchards that surrounded it provided the city with all its fruit. This abundance has left its mark on some of the dishes of the classic cuisine, as in this dish which combines the richness of duck with the tart cherries that still grow in Montmorency, on the outskirts of Paris.

Preparation time: 30 minutes
Cooking time: 1¾ hours
Oven temperature: 425°; reduced to 375°
To serve: 4 to 6

1 large dressed duck, with giblets
salt
freshly ground black pepper
1 onion, quartered
1 carrot, quartered
1 bouquet garni
2 pints tart or Morello cherries, pitted
juice of ½ lemon
3 tablespoons brandy or marc
2 tablespoons sugar
2 tablespoons red wine vinegar
¾ cup white wine
3 tablespoons butter
¼ cup flour

Wipe the duck well inside and out and season it generously with salt and pepper all over. Prick the skin with a sharp-pronged fork and place in a roasting pan. Roast for 15 minutes, then lower the oven temperature and roast for a further 1¼ hours, or until the juice that runs out when you prick the thickest part of the drumstick with a sharp-pronged fork is just clear. Pour off the fat from time to time.

Meanwhile, make a stock by simmering the duck giblets, onion, carrot and bouquet garni in water.

Marinate the cherries in the lemon juice and brandy or marc.

Put the sugar and vinegar into a small heavy saucepan and stir over a moderate heat to dissolve the sugar. Bring to a boil and allow the vinegar to evaporate. Remove from the heat when the mixture is just turning dark brown; do not allow it to burn. Add ¾ cup of the strained giblet stock and stir to dissolve the caramel.

When the duck is cooked, carve it into serving pieces and keep warm on a heated serving dish. Pour off excess fat from the roasting pan, add the wine to the pan and bring to a boil, stirring well to amalgamate any sediment. Add the caramelized stock and the marinating liquid from the cherries. Boil rapidly for a few minutes to reduce a little.

Work 2 tablespoons of the butter with the flour into a beurre manié and add to the sauce. Stir until smooth and simmer until the sauce thickens. Add the last piece of butter to give the sauce a glaze.

Add the cherries to the sauce and allow them to heat through. Pour the sauce carefully over and around the duck and serve very hot.

Poulet A La Comtoise

Chicken with Cheese
FRANCHE-COMTÉ

The creamily melting cheese of the Franche-Comté makes this a most luxurious dish, while the ingredients are very simple.

Preparation time: 40 minutes
Cooking time: 1½ hours
Oven temperature: 450°
To serve: 6 to 8

1 large roaster chicken, trussed
salt
freshly ground black pepper
½ cup+2 tablespoons butter
3 carrots, chopped
2 leeks, white parts only, thinly sliced
2 celery stalks, thinly sliced
about 1½ quarts boiling water
½ lb button mushrooms
¼ cup flour
¾ cup crème fraîche (see page 118)
1 egg yolk
juice of ½ lemon
pinch of grated nutmeg
1 cup shredded Comté or Gruyère cheese

Coq au vin au Riesling and poulet à la Comtoise

Wipe the chicken and season well with salt and pepper inside and out. Melt ¼ cup of the butter in a flameproof casserole and when foaming, add the chicken. Cover the pot and let the chicken color slowly, turning it over frequently so that it is buttery and uniformly light golden brown all over. Do not let the butter darken. Remove the chicken and set aside.

Add the carrots, leeks and celery to the casserole and cook gently until softened.

Return the chicken to the casserole, placing it on top of the bed of vegetables. Pour on enough boiling water to cover the chicken. Cover and simmer for about 1 hour.

Melt 2 tablespoons of the butter in a small saucepan and cook the mushrooms for 5 minutes over a quite high heat, so that they do not lose their moisture. Set aside.

When the chicken is cooked, remove it from the casserole, place in an ovenproof serving dish and keep warm. Strain the cooking liquid and boil very rapidly to reduce to about 3½ cups. Pass the vegetables through a blender or food processor.

Meanwhile work the flour into the remaining butter to make a beurre manié. Mix the cream into the egg yolk and stir in the lemon juice to make a smooth sauce.

When the stock has reduced sufficiently, strain it again into another clean saucepan and add the vegetable purée. Stir until smooth. Add the beurre manié, a little at a time, until it is all incorporated, and bring briefly to a boil. Remove from the heat and add the egg and cream mixture. Adjust the seasoning and add the nutmeg.

Sprinkle the chicken with half the cheese and press it in firmly. Surround with the mushrooms and gently pour over the sauce, so that the chicken becomes lightly coated as well as surrounded by the sauce. Sprinkle with the remaining cheese and place in the preheated oven. Cook for 15 minutes or until the top is golden brown and lightly crusted. Serve straight from the oven and carve at the table.

Oie Braisée A L'Alsacienne *Braised Goose with Sauerkraut*

Goose – roast, braised or preserved – can be found on menus everywhere in Alsace and Lorraine. The sauerkraut in this recipe, which is a typically Alsatian way of cooking goose, counteracts the richness of the bird; duck is also very good cooked in the same way.

Preparation time: 30 minutes
Cooking time: 2½ hours minimum
Oven temperature: 375°
To serve: 8 to 10

1 young dressed goose, trussed
salt
freshly ground black pepper
1 lb bulk pork sausage meat
2 large onions, finely chopped
3 lb sauerkraut, rinsed and drained
1 bouquet garni (bay leaf and thyme and
    rosemary sprigs)
12 juniper berries, lightly crushed
1 lb smoked pork
1¼ cups white wine
¼ cup butter
1 tablespoon oil

Remove the layers of fat from inside the goose. Season the goose well with salt and pepper inside and out and stuff it with the sausage meat, seasoned to taste.

Melt the goose fat in a large flameproof casserole, add the onions and sauerkraut and turn over a medium heat to coat evenly with a little fat. Add the bouquet garni, juniper berries and a little salt and pepper and bury the piece of smoked pork in the center. Add half the wine and enough water to come halfway up the sauerkraut. Bring to a boil, cover and simmer for at least 2½ hours, checking from time to time that the mixture is not getting too dry. Add a little water if necessary.

If you have a casserole large enough to hold the goose (or if you are cooking duck in this recipe) melt the butter with the oil in it and brown the goose on all sides. Add the remaining wine, cover and cook over a medium heat for at least 2 hours, or until the goose is cooked.

If the bird is too large to fit into a casserole, brush it with melted fat and cook on a rack in a roasting pan in the oven.

When the goose is cooked, carve it into serving pieces and keep warm. Skim the fat off the cooking juices.

Remove the piece of smoked pork from the casserole and carve it into thick slices.

Pile the sauerkraut into the center of a heated large, deep serving platter. Surround with the slices of smoked pork, and top with the pieces of goose. Pour on the cooking juices from the goose and serve very hot.

Oie braisée à l'Alsacienne

Faisan A La Vigneronne *Pheasant with Grapes*

BURGUNDY

This is a dish to celebrate the end of the grape harvest.

Preparation time: 30 minutes
Cooking time: about 1¼ hours
Oven temperature: 350°
To serve: 4

1 plump pheasant, plucked, drawn and
    trussed
salt
freshly ground black pepper
½ cup+2 tablespoons butter
1 carrot, chopped
1 onion, chopped
1¼ cups Chablis or other dry white wine
4 slices of white bread
1 pheasant liver
4 chicken livers
1 tablespoon brandy, warmed
¾ cup crème fraîche (see page 118)
1 cup purple grapes, peeled and seeded
1 cup seedless green grapes, peeled

Season the pheasant inside and out generously. Melt ¼ cup of the butter in a flameproof casserole, add the pheasant and brown lightly on all sides. Lift it out of the casserole. Spread the carrot and onion on the bottom of the casserole and place the pheasant on top. Moisten with a little of the wine. Cover the casserole and place in the oven. Cook for 45 to 55 minutes, basting from time to time and adding a little more butter if the pheasant seems to be getting too dry.

Melt ¼ cup of the remaining butter in a skillet and quickly brown the pieces of bread on both sides. Remove and keep warm.

Add the pheasant liver and chicken livers to the skillet and cook until they change color. Pour on the warmed brandy, set alight and leave until the flames die down.

Remove the livers from the skillet to a cold plate and mash them with a fork. Mash in the remaining butter and spread this mixture on the pieces of fried bread.

When the pheasant is ready, take it out of the casserole and cut into four pieces. Place on a heated serving dish and keep warm. Pour half the remaining wine into the casserole and the other half into the skillet. Bring to a boil, stirring well to remove any sediment on the bottom. Pour the wine from the skillet into the casserole, and continue to boil for a few minutes to reduce. Stir in the cream, season to taste with salt and pepper and heat through.

Surround the pheasant with the grapes and the pieces of fried bread. Pour over the sauce and serve very hot.

Coq Au Vin *Chicken Cooked in Red Burgundy Wine*

BURGUNDY

This is one of the classic dishes of French cooking, to be made for Sundays and holidays, using excellent ingredients. Use a large plump roaster or capon, a really good bottle of red Burgundy and some tasty field mushrooms or cèpes.

The dish needs no accompaniment other than a bottle of the wine in which it has been cooked, and it may be followed by a green salad.

Preparation time: 30 minutes
Cooking time: 1 to 1½ hours
To serve: 6 to 8

1 large roaster chicken or capon, cut up, or
    6 to 8 chicken pieces
2 tablespoons flour
salt
freshly ground black pepper
7 tablespoons butter
¼ lb Canadian bacon, diced
1 onion, quartered
1 carrot, quartered
¼ cup brandy
2½ cups red Burgundy wine
1 garlic clove, lightly crushed
1 bouquet garni
1 sugar cube
2 tablespoons oil
1 lb small onions, peeled
pinch of sugar
1 teaspoon wine vinegar
½ lb button mushrooms
6 slices of white bread, crusts removed

Dredge the chicken pieces with 1 tablespoon of the flour, liberally seasoned with salt and pepper.

Melt 2 tablespoons of the butter in a flameproof casserole, add the bacon, quartered onion and carrot and fry gently until the bacon begins to change color. Add the chicken pieces, raise the heat and fry until golden brown on all sides.

Heat the brandy in a small saucepan, set it alight and pour over the chicken, shaking the pan so that all the chicken pieces are covered in flames. When the flames have subsided, pour on the wine and stir to remove any sediment from the bottom of the casserole. Add the garlic, bouquet garni and sugar cube. Bring to a boil, then cover and simmer very gently until the chicken is tender. Test by pricking the thickest part of a drumstick; the chicken is done when the juice runs out clear.

Meanwhile, melt another 2 tablespoons of the butter with ½ tablespoon of the oil in a skillet. Add the small onions and fry until they begin to brown. Add the pinch of sugar and the vinegar, together with 1 tablespoon of the chicken cooking liquid. Cover and simmer for 10 to 15 minutes or until just tender. Keep warm.

Melt 2 tablespoons of the butter with ½ tablespoon of the oil in a heavy saucepan that is wide enough to hold the mushrooms lying flat. Raise the heat and add the mushrooms. Cook until they are crisp and browned. Keep warm.

When cooked, lift the chicken pieces out of the casserole and place in a deep heated serving dish. Surround with the small onions and mushrooms and keep hot.

Discard the bouquet garni. Skim the excess fat off the cooking liquid and put it into a skillet. Boil the liquid in the casserole briskly to reduce for 3 to 5 minutes.

Add the remaining oil to the fat in the skillet and quickly fry the pieces of bread until golden brown on both sides. Cut each slice into triangles.

Work the remaining flour into the remaining butter. Take the casserole off the heat and add the beurre manié in small pieces to the cooking liquid. Stir until smooth, then bring just to a boil. The sauce should now be quite thick and shiny. Adjust the seasoning and pour over the chicken. Garnish with the triangles of fried bread.

Poulet A L'Estragon *Tarragon Chicken*

BURGUNDY

To get the full flavor this dish should only be made with fresh French tarragon.

Preparation time: 20 minutes
Cooking time: 45 to 50 minutes
To serve: 4 to 6

4 to 6 fresh tarragon branches
about 2 teaspoons sea salt
about 1 teaspoon coarsely ground black
  pepper
1 roaster chicken, cut up, or 4 to 6 chicken
  pieces
6 tablespoons butter
½ lb small onions, peeled
½ bottle of dry white wine
1 bouquet garni

Strip the leaves off the tarragon and chop them fairly finely. Mix with the salt and pepper and roll each chicken piece in this mixture, pressing the mixture in quite firmly.

Melt the butter in a wide flameproof casserole and when it is foaming add the chicken pieces. Brown quickly on both sides to a light golden brown. Remove the chicken pieces from the casserole and keep warm.

Add the onions to the casserole and brown lightly. Take out and set aside.

Return the chicken pieces to the casserole, as far as possible laying them side by side on the bottom of the casserole, skin side down. Tuck the onions into any spaces between. Pour on the wine and bring to a boil. Add the bouquet garni, cover the casserole and lower the heat so that the liquid is only barely simmering. Cook for 40 to 45 minutes.

Test the chicken by pricking a drumstick with a fork or skewer; the liquid that runs out should be just clear, and the chicken will be moist and tender. Discard the bouquet garni before serving.

Poulet De Bresse Rôti *Roast Bresse Chicken*

BURGUNDY

The yellow corn-fed "poulets de Bresse" are famous throughout France as the plumpest and tastiest of chickens. This method of roasting shows the care taken by the French housewife with even the simplest process, and produces a moist, tender roast chicken, with crisp, golden brown skin.

Preparation time: 15 minutes
Cooking time: 1 to 1¼ hours
Oven temperature: 425°; reduced to 375°

1 large roaster chicken, with giblets
1 garlic clove, halved
salt
freshly ground black pepper
1 teaspoon dried or finely chopped fresh
  mixed herbs
½ cup butter, softened
1 onion, quartered
1 carrot, quartered
1 bouquet garni
strip of lemon rind
1 teaspoon flour

Wipe the chicken inside and out and rub first with the cut surface of the clove of garlic and then with salt and pepper and the herbs. Put a small pat of the butter inside the cavity.

Lay the chicken on its side on a rack in the roasting pan and smear the uppermost side liberally with some of the softened butter. Roast in the preheated oven for 15 minutes. Turn the chicken over and rub the side that is now uppermost with half of the remaining butter. Return to the oven. After another 15 minutes roasting, turn it breast up and smear the breast with all but a pat of the remaining butter. Lower the oven temperature and roast for a further 30 to 40 minutes, basting frequently with the fat in the pan.

Meanwhile put the giblets, onion, carrot, bouquet garni and lemon rind in a saucepan, cover with water and bring to a boil. Leave to simmer while the chicken is cooking.

Test to see if the chicken is cooked by piercing the thickest part of the drumstick: the chicken is ready when the juice that runs out is just clear. Remove it to a heated serving platter and keep warm, but do not return to the oven. The chicken should be left for at least 5 minutes, while you make the gravy, before carving.

Pour or skim off any excess fat from the roasting pan and bring the remaining juice to a boil. Strain in ¾ cup of the giblet stock and bring rapidly to a boil.

Make a beurre manié by working the flour into the remaining butter and add to the roasting pan off the heat. Stir to make a smooth sauce, adjust the seasoning and bring to a boil. Simmer for 1 minute, then strain into a heated sauceboat to serve with the chicken.

Coq au vin (page 61),
poulet de Bresse rôti and poulet à l'estragon

Poulet Basque *Chicken with Pepper and Tomatoes*

BEARN

Ideally, this dish should be made with some *piments basque* which are not quite as hot as chili peppers, but are a good deal spicier than the ordinary pimiento. If these are not obtainable, add one chili pepper or paprika.

Preparation time: 20 minutes
Cooking time: 1 hour
To serve: 4 to 6

1 roaster chicken, cut up, or 4 to 6 chicken
   pieces
salt
freshly ground black pepper
$\frac{1}{4}$ cup goose or pork fat, or lard
2 large onions, thinly sliced
4 garlic cloves, finely chopped
1 lb highly spiced basque or Spanish-type
   sausage, or salami, in one piece
2 green peppers, cored, seeded and sliced
2 hot red chili peppers, seeded and sliced, or
   1 sweet red pepper, cored, seeded and sliced,
   and 1 tablespoon paprika
1 lb tomatoes, peeled and seeded
1 to 1$\frac{1}{2}$ cups long grain rice

Season the chicken pieces with salt and pepper. Melt the fat or lard in a flameproof casserole and brown the chicken pieces quickly on all sides. Remove from the pot and set aside.

Add the onions and garlic to the casserole and sweat until soft. Lay the chicken pieces on top of the vegetables and add enough water to come halfway up the chicken. Bring to a boil, then cover and simmer gently for about 15 minutes.

Add the sausage or salami, green peppers, chili peppers, or red pepper and paprika, and the tomatoes. Re-cover and simmer until the chicken is tender. Adjust the seasoning.

Just before the chicken is done, cook the rice in boiling salted water for about 10 minutes until almost cooked. Drain and place in a shallow flameproof casserole or heavy saucepan. Pour over some of the chicken cooking liquid and simmer until the rice is tender and has absorbed most of the chicken liquid.

Serve by piling the rice onto a heated deep serving dish, or leave in the casserole in which it has cooked. Lay the pieces of chicken on top, together with the sausage cut into chunks and pour over the vegetable mixture and stock. Serve very hot.

Oie Farcie Aux Pruneaux *Goose Stuffed with Prunes*

GUYENNE

The town of Agen in the center of the Guyenne is famous for its plums and prunes. These are not only stuffed to make a special confectionery but also used a great deal in cooking savory dishes. Combined with goose they make an exceptionally rich and delicious meal.

Preparation time: 30 minutes (plus soaking
   overnight)
Cooking time: 2 to 2$\frac{1}{2}$ hours
Oven temperature: 425°; reduced to 350°
To serve: 8

9 to 10 lb dressed goose, with the diced
   liver
salt
freshly ground black pepper
1 lb prunes, soaked overnight
1$\frac{1}{4}$ cups white wine
3 tablespoons butter
1 tablespoon finely chopped shallots
2 tablespoons port or brandy
2 cups soft white bread crumbs
1 small can pâté de foie gras (optional)
1 teaspoon flour

Rub the goose inside and out liberally with salt and pepper and prick the skin all over so that the fat runs out easily.

Drain the prunes and put them in a saucepan with the wine. Bring to a boil and simmer for about 10 minutes, or until tender. Drain, reserving the cooking liquid. Pit the prunes and chop finely.

Melt 2 tablespoons of the butter in a skillet, add the shallots and fry until softened. Add the goose liver and cook for 3 minutes or until it just begins to change color. Remove the liver and shallot mixture to a bowl.

Add the port or brandy to the skillet and bring quickly to a boil, stirring to loosen any sediment. Pour into the bowl. Stir in the bread crumbs, pâté de foie gras, if used, and the prunes. Stuff the goose with this mixture.

Place the goose on a rack in a large roasting pan and put in the oven. Lower the temperature after 15 minutes and continue to roast, pouring off the fat occasionally.

When the goose is cooked (test by pricking the thickest part of the drumstick with a skewer – the juice that runs out should be just clear) remove to a heated serving dish. Pour or skim off the remaining fat from the roasting pan, leaving the meat juices. Sprinkle in the flour, stir until smooth and cook gently for 1 minute. Add the prune cooking liquid and bring quickly to a boil, stirring well. Taste the sauce for seasoning, and add the remaining butter, cut into small pieces, to give the sauce a glaze. Pour into a heated sauceboat and serve with the goose.

Meats

Carbonnade De Boeuf Flamande *Beef Braised in Beer*

FLANDERS

The influence of Belgium in this part of France makes itself felt in the frequent use of beer in cooking, as in this sustaining dish to be served on cold days, with baked potatoes or noodles.

Preparation time: 20 minutes
Cooking time: 2½ to 3 hours
Oven temperature: 300°
To serve: 6

2 lb beef for stew, trimmed and cubed
salt
freshly ground black pepper
¼ cup butter or beef drippings
1 lb onions, sliced
2 tablespoons flour
1 teaspoon brown sugar
1 tablespoon wine vinegar
2½ cups dark beer or stout
1 bouquet garni

Season the meat generously with salt and pepper. Melt the butter or drippings in a flameproof casserole and quickly brown the pieces of meat on all sides. Remove and set aside.

Add the onions to the casserole, lower the heat and fry until golden brown. Remove from the casserole and set aside.

Sprinkle the flour into the casserole and cook over a moderately high heat, stirring well, until it is dark golden brown. Add the sugar and vinegar, and when the vinegar has evaporated, add the beer slowly, stirring well to loosen any sediment on the bottom of the casserole, and to make a smooth sauce.

Return the meat and onions to the casserole in alternate layers, add the bouquet garni and bring back to a boil. Cover and cook in the oven until the meat is very tender and the sauce has thickened. You can also simmer the carbonnade over a low heat on top of the stove.

Remove the bouquet garni before serving, and serve very hot.

Hochepot *Boiled Beef with Vegetables*

FLANDERS

The authentic recipe for this sturdy country dish includes a piece of pig's head with the ear, but for less robust appetites a piece of the thick end of fresh pork sides will make a very nice substitute. The sausage should be a really good meaty, uncooked and coarse country sausage, preferably French, but could also be Belgian or German.

Preparation time: 20 minutes
Cooking time: 3 hours
To serve: 6 to 8

2 tablespoons butter or lard
about 2 lb piece of fresh beef, brisket or
   flank steak, boned and rolled
1 cup water
1 lb fresh pork sides, lean end
½ lb piece of sausage (see above)
6 carrots, peeled or scraped
6 turnips, peeled
6 leeks
1 white cabbage, quartered and cored
½ teaspoon ground allspice
salt
freshly ground black pepper

Melt the butter or lard in a large flameproof casserole or Dutch oven and brown the pieces of beef on all sides. Add the water and bring to a boil. Cover and simmer for 1 hour, then add the pork, and continue cooking for another hour. At the end of this time, skim excess fat off the surface of the cooking liquid, and add the sausage, vegetables, allspice and salt and pepper to taste. Cover and simmer for a further hour.

Lift out the meat and sausage and place on a large heated serving dish. Carve them into thick slices. Surround with the vegetables and serve very hot.

Boeuf À La Bourguignonne *Beef Stewed in Burgundy Wine*

BURGUNDY

Made with tender Charollais beef and a good Burgundy wine, this is the richest and most satisfying of all the beef casseroles.

Preparation time: 30 minutes
Cooking time: 3 hours
Oven temperature: 300°
To serve: 6 to 8

3 lb beef chuck or top round steak, cubed
¼ cup flour
salt
freshly ground black pepper
½ cup + 2 tablespoons butter
3 tablespoons olive oil
2 tablespoons brandy
1 bottle of red Burgundy wine
¼ lb slab bacon, finely diced
2 onions, finely chopped
2 carrots, finely chopped
2 garlic cloves, finely chopped
1 bouquet garni (bay leaf and thyme, parsley and fennel sprigs)
1 lb small onions, peeled
1 teaspoon sugar
1 teaspoon wine vinegar
1 tablespoon water
1 lb button mushrooms

Dredge the cubes of beef in the flour, which has been liberally seasoned with salt and pepper, so that they all become evenly coated. Melt half the butter with the olive oil in a heavy skillet. When very hot put in just as much of the beef as will cover the bottom of the pan. Fry quickly, turning, until all the beef cubes are golden brown and lightly crusted all over. Remove from the skillet to a flame-proof casserole. Brown the remaining beef cubes in the same way.

Pour the brandy into the skillet. Stir well to remove any sediment and allow to bubble fiercely for 1 minute. Add as much wine as the pan will hold and bring to a boil. Allow to boil for 1 minute, then pour all the wine over the meat. The liquid should come just level with the meat – add a little water if necessary.

Melt 1 tablespoon of the butter in the skillet and quickly fry the bacon, chopped onions, carrots and garlic until just turning golden brown. Add to the casserole, together with the bouquet garni. Cover the casserole and place in the oven, or leave to simmer, half covered, over a very low heat on top of the stove. Cook for 2 hours.

Melt half the remaining butter in the skillet and quickly brown the small onions. Just as they begin to turn golden brown, sprinkle with the sugar, add the vinegar and water and cook for another minute to allow the moisture to evaporate. Add to the casserole and continue to cook for another hour.

Just before the casserole is ready to serve, cook the mushrooms very quickly in the remaining butter. Add the mushrooms to the casserole and adjust the seasoning before serving.

Entrecôtes Bourguignonnes *Steak Cooked in Red Wine*

BURGUNDY

This dish combines all the best ingredients of the area – the tender beef of the Charollais cattle, the full-bodied red wines and the abundant field mushrooms.

Preparation time: 15 minutes
Cooking time: 15 to 20 minutes
To serve: 4

4 steaks
salt
freshly ground black pepper
½ cup butter
1 tablespoon oil
1 tablespoon finely chopped shallots
1¼ cups red Burgundy wine
1 cup thinly sliced mushrooms
½ tablespoon finely chopped fresh parsley

Season the steaks on both sides. Melt half the butter with the oil in a heavy skillet. When very hot, add the steaks and cook quickly on both sides to the desired degree of doneness. Remove from the pan and keep hot on a heated serving platter.

Add the shallots to the skillet and cook for a few minutes, until they are soft but not colored. Add the wine, bring rapidly to a boil and allow to reduce to about half.

Meanwhile melt half the remaining butter in a heavy saucepan, add the mushrooms and cook rapidly until tender. Add the mushrooms to the shallots and bring to a boil again, then remove from the heat. Adjust the seasoning and add the remaining butter, cut into small pieces, to give the sauce a glaze.

Pour the sauce over the steaks, sprinkle with the parsley and serve very hot.

Queue De Boeuf A La Bourguignonne *Oxtail Stewed in Red Wine*

BURGUNDY

True to the French housewifely tradition, no part of the animal is wasted, and oxtail is cooked in numerous ways. This is one of the simplest, and the only extravagant ingredient is a bottle of good Burgundy wine. As it needs such long slow cooking, the dish is not worth making in small quantities.

Preparation time: 30 minutes (plus soaking)
Cooking time: about 4 hours
Oven temperature: 300°
To serve: 8 to 10

2 oxtails, thickly sliced
¼ lb slab bacon or smoked pork, diced
2 onions, chopped
4 carrots, sliced
1 bouquet garni
salt
freshly ground black pepper
1 bottle of red Burgundy wine
pinch of sugar

Soak the oxtail in cold water for a few hours. Drain well.

Fry the bacon or pork in its own fat in a flameproof casserole. When the fat begins to run, raise the heat, add the pieces of oxtail and brown on all sides. Remove the oxtail and add the onions and carrots to the casserole. Cook until just coloring.

Place the pieces of oxtail on top of the vegetables and add the bouquet garni and salt and pepper to taste.

Bring the wine quickly to a boil with the sugar, then pour over the oxtail in the casserole. Bring to a boil again, cover and place in the oven. Cook until the meat is very tender.

Skim off excess fat from the top of the casserole and adjust the seasoning before serving.

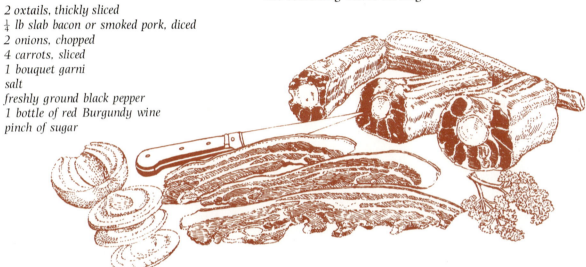

Entrecôtes A La Moutarde *Steak with Mustard Sauce*

BURGUNDY

Nothing could be simpler, or better, than a tender steak, cooked with this deceptively smooth sauce.

Preparation time: 10 minutes
Cooking time: 10 to 15 minutes
To serve: 4

4 steaks
salt
freshly ground black pepper
¼ cup butter
1 tablespoon oil
1 tablespoon Dijon-style mustard
2 tablespoons crème fraîche (see page 118)
   or heavy cream

Season the steaks on both sides. Melt the butter with the oil in a heavy skillet. When very hot, add the steaks and cook on both sides to the desired degree of doneness. Remove from the pan and keep hot on a heated serving platter.

Add the mustard and cream to the skillet, stir until smooth and bring just to a boil. Adjust the seasoning, pour over the steaks and serve.

Tournedos Rossini *Steak with Pâté de Foie Gras*

ILE DE FRANCE

An incredibly sumptuous dish, this is said to have been invented by the composer himself. If you were to have it in one of the best Paris restaurants, it would be made not only with foie gras truffé, but would probably come topped with a slice of fresh truffle as well. You can, however, make a perfectly good, slightly less extravagant version yourself, using the best pâté de foie gras you can, preferably homemade (see page 38).

Preparation time: 10 minutes
Cooking time: 20 to 25 minutes
To serve: 4

4 boneless sirloin steaks
1 garlic clove, halved
salt
freshly ground black pepper
$\frac{1}{4}$ cup butter
1 tablespoon oil
4 slices of white bread
4 slices of pâté de foie gras
2 tablespoons white wine
watercress to garnish

Prepare the steaks by rubbing each side with the cut surface of the clove of garlic and salt and pepper.

Melt half the butter with half the oil in a heavy skillet and quickly brown the slices of bread on both sides. Place each on a heated plate and keep warm.

Add the remaining butter and oil to the skillet and heat until frothing, then add the steaks. Cook for 6 to 8 minutes on each side, to the desired degree of doneness. Place each steak on top of its croûton of fried bread. Top with a piece of pâté, which should melt a little from the heat of the steak. Keep warm.

Pour the wine into the skillet and allow to bubble while scraping up any sediment from the bottom of the pan. Pour a little of this sauce over the top of each steak and serve immediately, garnished only with watercress.

Entrecôtes Bourguignonne, entrecôtes à la moutarde, and bouef à la Bourguignonne

70

Tournedos Rossini, filet de bouef en croute and petits pois à la Française (page 103)

Filet De Boeuf En Croûte

Beef Tenderloin in a Pastry Case
ILE DE FRANCE

This dish belongs to the realms of haute cuisine, but it is not difficult to produce at home for special occasions.

Preparation time: 30 minutes (plus pastry)
Cooking time: 30 to 35 minutes
Oven temperature: 425°; reduced to 375°
To serve: 8 or more

about 2 lb piece beef tenderloin
1 garlic clove, halved
2 tablespoons brandy
salt
freshly ground black pepper
6 tablespoons butter
1 large mild onion, finely chopped
1 cup finely chopped mushrooms
about ½ quantity pâte feuilletée (see
   page 115) or puff pastry
1 egg yolk
1 tablespoon water

Rub the beef all over first with the cut surface of the clove of garlic, then with 1 tablespoon of the brandy, and then with salt and pepper. Melt half the butter in a heavy skillet, and when it is foaming, put in the beef and sear it quickly on all sides. Take out and leave to cool.

Add the remaining butter to the skillet and cook the onion and mushrooms together until soft. Add the remaining brandy, raise the heat and allow to bubble fiercely until almost all the liquid has evaporated. Leave to cool.

Divide the pastry into two parts, roughly one-third and two-thirds. Roll out the smaller piece to form a rectangle. Line a baking sheet with foil lightly buttered on both sides, and lay the pastry rectangle on top. Spread half the cooled mushroom mixture over the center, lay the beef on top and cover it with the remaining mushroom mixture.

Roll out the remaining pastry to form a larger rectangle. Place it carefully over the top of the beef and then seal the edges well to make a neat package. Decorate with leaves made from leftover scraps of pastry. Brush with the egg yolk mixed with the water. Cook in the preheated oven for 20 minutes, then lower the oven temperature and cook for a further 10 to 15 minutes. The pastry should have risen on top and be golden brown. The meat inside should be just cooked *à point*: pale brown on the outside and pink in the center.

Serve whole, and slice thickly at the table.

Note: If you do not like your beef rare, pre-cook the meat in the hot oven for 10 minutes instead of sealing it in the skillet.

71

Boeuf En Daube Provençale *Casserole of Beef with Wine and Herbs*

PROVENCE

This is one of those age-old country recipes which originally would have been taken to the village baker for long slow cooking in his oven after the bread-baking is over. The meat must cook so slowly that it emerges tender enough to be eaten with a spoon, and although the casserole should be sealed, a quite irresistible aroma of wine and herbs will steal out during the course of the cooking.

Preparation time: 30 minutes
Cooking time: 4 to 5 hours
Oven temperature: 275°
To serve: 6 to 8

1 tablespoon olive oil
½ lb salt pork or slab bacon, diced
2 onions, sliced
2 carrots, sliced
2 garlic cloves, finely chopped
2¼ lb chuck steak, trimmed of fat and cut
    into large cubes
2½ cups red wine
2 sprigs each of fresh thyme, rosemary and
    parsley
1 bay leaf
2 strips of orange rind
3 tomatoes, peeled and roughly chopped
salt
freshly ground black pepper
½ cup pitted ripe olives

Heat the oil in a flameproof casserole, add the salt pork or bacon and fry until transparent. Add the onions, carrots and garlic and continue frying until softened. Raise the heat, add the meat and brown on all sides.

Bring the wine to a boil in a separate saucepan and boil fiercely for 5 minutes. Pour it over the meat and add the herbs, orange rind, tomatoes and salt and pepper to taste. Cover tightly with a double thickness of foil and then the lid of the casserole and transfer to the oven. Cook for 4 to 5 hours. Add the olives to the dish 5 minutes before serving.

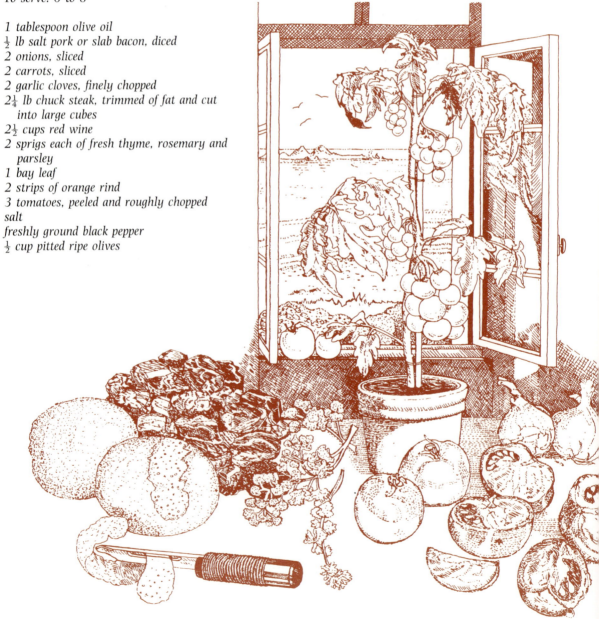

Boeuf A La Mode *Cold Jellied Beef*

ILE DE FRANCE

This is a beautiful dish when carefully made – tender, larded beef in a clear dark aspic, surrounded by bright carrots; the perfect dish for a buffet table, especially as it is made with a large piece of beef, and has to be prepared at least a day ahead.

Preparation time: about 40 minutes (plus setting overnight and chilling)
Cooking time: about 5 hours
Oven temperature: 275°
To serve: 12 or more

5 to $5\frac{1}{2}$ lb piece of rolled, boned beef, such as rump or eye of round
$\frac{1}{4}$ lb piece of pork fat
salt
freshly ground black pepper
$\frac{1}{2}$ teaspoon mixed dried herbs
2 garlic cloves, one very finely chopped
$\frac{1}{4}$ cup butter
2 onions, sliced
$\frac{3}{4}$ cup brandy
$2\frac{1}{2}$ cups red wine
1 calf's foot or 2 pig's feet, split and blanched
1 bouquet garni (bay leaf and thyme, rosemary and parsley sprigs)
1 strip of orange rind
$2\frac{1}{2}$ lb carrots
broth or water
a little lemon juice

Garnish
parsley sprigs
lemon slices

If the beef is rolled in fat, remove the outer wrapping of fat. Ask the butcher to lard the beef for you, if possible. If not, season the piece of pork fat with plenty of salt and pepper, the herbs and chopped garlic, cut it into strips and use to thread through the meat at intervals using a larding needle.

Melt the butter in a flameproof casserole which is large enough to hold the meat. Add the onions and soften them. Raise the heat, add the piece of meat and brown it quickly on all sides.

Pour in the warmed brandy and set alight. When the flames have died down, pour in the wine. Fit the calf's foot or pig's feet around the meat, add the bouquet garni, some more seasoning, the orange rind, the whole garlic clove and one carrot cut in half. Add enough broth or water just to cover the meat. Bring to a boil.

Remove from the heat and cover the pot with a very well-fitting lid. Seal the lid with a flour and water paste. Transfer the casserole to the oven and leave to cook for 4 to 5 hours, depending on the size of the meat.

Take the casserole out of the oven and leave to cool a little. Unseal the lid and lift out the meat. It should not have lost its shape but should be very tender. Transfer the meat to another dish, cover well and refrigerate overnight.

Strain the stock and taste it for seasoning. Refrigerate overnight. The calf's foot or pig's feet may be eaten now on their own.

The next day, remove the lid of fat that will have set on top of the stock. The stock underneath should have set to a light jelly. If it has not set sufficiently, it may be boiled for some minutes to reduce; a little gelatin can also be used to help the setting, but usually this is not necessary. Melt down the jellied stock and add a little lemon juice and more seasoning if necessary. Leave to cool.

Cook the remaining carrots, left whole if they are young and small, cut lengthwise into halves or quarters if not, in boiling salted water until just tender. Drain and cool.

Slice the meat thickly – although very tender, it should be possible to slice it neatly with a really sharp carving knife once the meat has been chilled and left to set overnight. Arrange the slices of meat in a large serving dish, at least 2 inches deep. Surround with the carrots. When the stock is cool but has not yet begun to set, pour it carefully over the meat and carrots. Chill for several hours until set before serving, garnished with sprigs of parsley and slices of lemon.

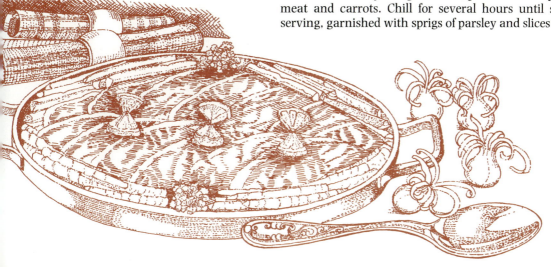

Carbonnade Nîmoise

Lamb Baked with Potatoes and Eggplants
LANGUEDOC

This is an economical and filling dish from the Languedoc, an area that is perhaps less exuberant in its cooking than Provence, but famous for several of the more substantial dishes of the classic French *cuisine bourgeoise*. The proportion of meat to vegetables, and of the vegetables to each other, can be adjusted to suit individual appetites and what is available: it is the long slow cooking of meat and vegetables together which gives the dish its comforting richness of flavor.

Preparation time: 30 minutes (plus 1 hour
   for draining eggplants)
Cooking time: 3 hours
Oven temperature: 450°; reduced to 350°
To serve: 6 to 8

2 lb eggplants, diced
salt
1 leg of lamb, boned and cut into $\frac{1}{2}$ inch
   thick slices
2 garlic cloves, cut into slivers
freshly ground black pepper
2 tablespoons olive oil
$\frac{1}{4}$ lb slab bacon or salt pork, diced
2 lb potatoes, peeled and diced
1 teaspoon dried thyme
1 teaspoon dried marjoram

Put the eggplants in a colander, sprinkle liberally with salt and leave to drain for 1 hour.

Spike each lamb steak with one or two slivers of garlic. Season the lamb steaks on both sides with salt and pepper.

When the eggplants are ready, rinse them, squeeze out well and pat dry.

Heat the oil in a large roasting pan or large flat baking or gratin dish. Scatter on the bacon or salt pork and lay the lamb steaks on top. Cover with the potatoes and eggplants. Sprinkle on a little more salt and pepper and the herbs and place in the oven.

After 20 minutes baking, cover the pan or dish tightly with a double thickness of foil and lower the oven temperature. Cook for at least a further $2\frac{1}{2}$ hours. The dish may be left longer if convenient. Both meat and vegetables should be very tender, and all the liquid absorbed.

Serve hot.

Carbonnade Nimoise and
bouef en daube Provençale (page 72)

Gigot A La Couronne D'Ail

Leg of Lamb with a Crown of Garlic
CHARENTE

Recipes using the legendary *quarante gousses d'ail* appear all over the southern part of France where garlic grows in rich abundance. Garlic is sometimes served as a vegetable in its own right, especially in the summer when the crowns are first lifted, the skin is still moist and pliable and the cloves green tinged, fat and juicy.
This dish belongs to the coastal areas where the lambs feed on the reclaimed salt marshes, and garlic is grown. It must be made with the new season's garlic.

Preparation time: 20 minutes
Cooking time: $1\frac{1}{2}$ to 2 hours
Oven temperature: 425°; reduced to 375°
To serve: 6 to 8

40 or more garlic cloves
1 leg of lamb
$\frac{1}{4}$ cup olive oil
1 teaspoon dried thyme
1 teaspoon dried rosemary
salt
freshly ground black pepper
$\frac{3}{4}$ cup broth
juice of $\frac{1}{2}$ lemon
$\frac{1}{4}$ cup butter

Peel three of the garlic cloves and cut them into slivers. Using a sharp, pointed knife, make small incisions in the surface of the leg of lamb and insert a sliver of garlic in each. Place the lamb in a roasting pan.

Mix the olive oil with the herbs and salt and pepper and pour a little of the mixture over the leg of lamb. Place in the hot oven and after 15 minutes roasting, lower the temperature and baste the lamb with the remaining oil mixture. Continue roasting until the lamb is cooked, basting from time to time. The lamb should be still pink towards the center. Test by inserting a skewer – the lamb is cooked when the liquid which runs out is only just colorless.

Meanwhile, blanch the remaining garlic cloves, unpeeled, in boiling salted water for 10 minutes. Drain and place in a small saucepan with the broth. Bring to a boil and simmer gently for 20 minutes.

When the lamb is cooked, remove it from the roasting pan and place on a heated serving dish. Surround with the drained garlic cloves. Add the liquid in which the garlic has been simmering to the roasting juices in the pan and bring to a boil, stirring well to loosen any sediment. Season to taste with salt and pepper and add the lemon juice. Stir in the butter cut into small pieces to give the sauce a glaze, pour over the lamb and serve.

Gigot De Pré-Salé Aux Haricots Verts

Roast Lamb with Green Beans and Potatoes
BRITTANY

The salt meadows (*prés-salés*) of Northern Brittany, around St. Malo, are grazing grounds for the tender and delicately flavored lambs famous throughout France. A gigot, or roast leg of lamb, is usually served surrounded with local vegetables, and is always cooked to the point where it is still just pink and very juicy.

Preparation time: 30 minutes
Cooking time: about 1 hour
Oven temperature: 375°
To serve: 6 to 8

3½ lb leg of lamb
salt
freshly ground black pepper
2 garlic cloves, cut into slivers
¾ cup butter
1½ lb potatoes, peeled and chopped
2 lb green beans, stringed if necessary
½ cup white wine
½ cup water
2 tablespoons capers
12 juniper berries, roughly chopped

Rub the leg of lamb all over with salt and pepper, then spike it with the slivers of garlic. Place it in a roasting pan. Melt ¼ cup of the butter and pour it over the lamb. Roast in the oven, basting from time to time, for about 1 hour.

After 30 minutes, melt 6 tablespoons of the butter in a heavy skillet. When foaming, add the potato slices and turn well so that they each become coated with butter. Add salt and pepper to taste, then lower the heat, cover the pan and cook gently for 30 to 35 minutes or until tender. Stir occasionally to prevent the slices sticking.

When the lamb has been cooking for about 40 minutes, plunge the beans into a large saucepan of boiling salted water and cook rapidly, uncovered, for 15 to 20 minutes or until tender. Drain and keep warm.

After 1 hour, test the lamb to see if it is cooked by pricking with a skewer – it is ready when the liquid which spurts out is just colorless. Remove from the roasting pan and place on a heated deep serving dish. Keep warm.

Pour off the excess fat from the roasting pan. Add a little of the fat to the potatoes and raise the heat to brown them. Add the wine to the juices in the roasting pan. Bring quickly to a boil, scraping well to loosen any sediment. Stir in the water and bring back to a boil. Pour over the lamb.

Mix the capers and juniper berries into the potatoes and arrange them around the lamb alternately with the beans. Dot the beans with the remaining butter just before serving.

Epaule D'Agneau Aux Noix *Shoulder of Lamb with Walnuts*

MARCHE AND LIMOUSIN

Walnut trees grow to mature splendor in this part of France and walnuts and walnut oil are used a great deal in savory cooking, as well as for cakes and confectionery. They flavor vegetables, sausages and stuffings.

Preparation time: 20 minutes
Cooking time: 1¼ to 1½ hours
Oven temperature: 425°; reduced to 375°
To serve: 4 to 6

1 shoulder of lamb, boned
1 garlic clove, halved
salt and freshly ground black pepper
¼ cup butter
1 onion, finely chopped
½ lb fresh pork sides, skinned, boned and
    finely ground, or bulk sausage meat
8 walnuts, shelled and chopped
2 tablespoons finely chopped fresh parsley
finely grated rind of 1 orange
1 egg, beaten
¾ cup white wine

Rub the shoulder inside the cavity and on the outside with the cut surface of the garlic clove and season well with salt and pepper.

Melt half the butter in a skillet, add the onion and fry until softened. Add the pork or sausage meat and fry very quickly until the meat just begins to change color.

Turn out into a bowl, add the walnuts, parsley, orange rind and salt and pepper to taste and bind the mixture with the egg. Stuff into the cavity in the shoulder of lamb left by the bone. Place the shoulder on a rack in a roasting pan, dot with the remaining butter and place in the preheated oven.

After 15 minutes roasting, lower the oven temperature and continue to roast, basting from time to time, until the meat is cooked. Test by inserting a skewer: the juice that runs out should be only just colorless, and the meat should be pink but set in the center.

Place the meat on a heated serving dish and keep warm. Add the wine to the roasting pan and bring quickly to a boil, stirring well to loosen any sediment. Season to taste with salt and pepper and pour into a heated sauceboat. Serve the meat very hot, and slice at the table.

Navarin Printanier

Lamb Cooked with Spring Vegetables
BERRY

Paris is usually the first to enjoy the primeurs, the delicate young spring vegetables brought in from nearby market gardens at the peak of tender, youthful perfection. Bunches of bright orange carrots with frilly green foliage, pink-flushed baby turnips, waxy yellow new potatoes no bigger than a hen's egg, and juicy young peas – as soon as these arrive in the vegetable stalls, it is time to make a navarin.

Preparation time: 30 minutes
Cooking time: 1 to 1¼ hours
To serve: 6 to 8

¼ *cup butter*
2 onions, thinly sliced
2 garlic cloves, finely chopped
1 shoulder of lamb, boned and cut into cubes
2 tablespoons flour
1 teaspoon sugar
2½ cups broth or water
1 bouquet garni
salt
freshly ground black pepper
1 lb new potatoes, scrubbed or scraped
1 lb young carrots, scrubbed or scraped
1 lb small onions, peeled
1 lb baby turnips, scrubbed
1 lb (about 2 cups) shelled peas

Melt the butter in a flameproof casserole, add the sliced onions and garlic and fry until golden brown. Remove from the casserole.

Add the meat to the casserole and fry quickly, stirring to brown on all sides. Remove from the casserole.

Sprinkle the flour and sugar into the casserole and stir until it becomes dark brown, but not burnt. Add the broth or water slowly, stirring well, to obtain a smooth sauce.

Return the meat and onions to the casserole with the bouquet garni and salt and pepper to taste. Cover and simmer for 20 minutes.

Add the potatoes and carrots to the casserole. Re-cover and simmer for a further 10 minutes.

Add the small onions and turnips and continue to simmer, covered, for another 15 minutes.

Add the peas, raise the heat a little and cook, uncovered, until the peas are tender (about 10 minutes). The meat and all the other vegetables should be ready at about the same time – they must not be allowed to overcook and lose their shape. The sauce should be smooth and quite thin, but if it seems to be at all watery, you can add a little beurre manié – (a blended paste of flour and butter) to thicken it at the end. Adjust the seasoning before serving.

Jambon Persillé *Ham in Aspic*

BURGUNDY

One of the prettiest sights in the *charcuterie* windows in the Burgundy area, especially around Easter time, is the marbled pink and green jambon persillé, usually sold out of large white china bowls.

It is not worth making this dish in small quantities, but it is not difficult to prepare and is lovely on a summer table.

Preparation time: 30 minutes (plus setting overnight)
Cooking time: 4 hours minimum
To serve: 10 to 12

3 to 4½ lb piece uncooked, bone-in country
  ham (preferably unsmoked), scrubbed and
  soaked in cold water overnight
2 calf's or pig's feet
1 large bouquet garni (bay leaves and
  parsley, thyme and tarragon sprigs)
12 peppercorns
2 onions, quartered
1 bottle of dry white wine
2 teaspoons white wine vinegar
salt
freshly ground black pepper
1 cup finely chopped fresh parsley

Put the ham into a large saucepan, cover with cold water and bring very slowly to a boil. Pour off the water and rinse the pan and ham. Cover with cold water again and bring slowly to a boil. Simmer for 1 hour.

Drain and rinse the ham. When the ham is cool enough to handle, remove the rind if necessary and cut the meat off the bone into large pieces.

Blanch the calf's or pig's feet in boiling water and drain.

Put the ham pieces back into the clean saucepan, add the calf's or pig's feet, the bouquet garni, peppercorns, onions and wine. Add enough water to cover the meat. Bring slowly to a boil, then simmer for about 3 hours or until the meat is very tender. Skim any fat or scum off the cooking liquid from time to time.

When the ham is ready, lift it out of the saucepan. Strain the cooking liquid into another bowl. Add the vinegar to the liquid and adjust the seasoning. Leave to cool.

Mash the ham lightly with a fork and put into a large serving dish, preferably white to show off the pink and green of the finished dish.

When the cooking liquid begins to set into a jelly, skim off any fat that may have risen to the surface and stir in the parsley. Pour over the ham and leave to set overnight in the refrigerator.

You can serve the dish in its bowl or unmold it onto a platter.

Saupiquet Nivernais *Smoked Ham in Cream Sauce*

NIVERNAIS

Recipes for a saupiquet (from the verb meaning to spike with salt) can be traced back as far as the 16th century. This dish is quite sharp, so serve with boiled or mashed potatoes.

Preparation time: 25 minutes
Cooking time: 25 minutes
To serve: 4

½ cup butter
4 center-cut smoked ham slices
½ cup flour
¾ cup broth or water
¾ cup white wine
¼ cup wine vinegar
1 tablespoon finely chopped shallots
6 peppercorns, lightly crushed
6 juniper berries, lightly crushed
1¼ cups crème fraîche (see page 118)
salt
freshly ground black pepper
finely chopped fresh tarragon or parsley to
  garnish

Melt 7 tablespoons of the butter in a large skillet, add the ham slices and quickly sear on both sides. Remove from the pan and keep hot on a heated serving platter.

Sprinkle the flour into the skillet and cook, stirring, until the mixture begins to turn brown. Gradually stir in the broth or water then the wine. Stir until smooth, then bring to a boil and cook gently for 1 minute.

Put the vinegar into a small saucepan together with the shallots, peppercorns and juniper berries and bring quickly to a boil. Boil until reduced by half, then strain into the sauce in the skillet. Add the cream to the sauce and stir until very smooth. Adjust the seasoning.

Add the remaining butter, cut into small pieces, to give the sauce a glaze. Pour the sauce over the slices of ham, sprinkle with the tarragon or chives and serve hot.

Saupiquet Nivernaise and jambon persillé

Noisettes De Porc Aux Pruneaux De Tours *Pork Chops with Prunes*

TOURAINE

The Touraine is famous for its plump and juicy prunes, and Tours itself for the richness of its food. This sumptuous dish, which is a specialty of the town, is a feast to be eaten at leisure. It really should be made with the local petillant white Vouvray wine, but any good dry white wine will do. Do not expect to eat more than a little fruit to follow.

Preparation time: 20 minutes (plus soaking)
Cooking time: 30 to 45 minutes
To serve: 6 to 8

½ lb prunes
½ bottle of white Vouvray
6 to 8 pork cutlets or loin chops, boned
1 tablespoon flour
salt
freshly ground black pepper
¼ cup butter
1 tablespoon currant jelly
1¼ cups crème fraîche (see page 118)
squeeze of lemon juice

Soak the prunes in the wine for several hours, then simmer them very gently in the wine until soft. Drain the prunes, reserving the wine. Pit and chop them roughly.

Dredge the pork in the flour which has been liberally seasoned with salt and pepper. Melt the butter in a deep skillet and when it is frothing, add the pork. Cook over a moderate heat, turning once, until just golden on both sides but not browned. Add a tablespoon or two of the prune wine, cover and cook over a gentle heat until the pork is cooked – from 15 to 20 minutes, depending on the thickness of the cuts. When the pork is cooked, transfer it to a heated serving dish.

Add the remaining prune wine to the skillet, stir well to remove any sediment and bring to a boil. Boil to reduce to a thin syrupy consistency. Add the currant jelly and stir until melted, then add the crème fraîche little by little, stirring to amalgamate. Bring to a boil and boil until quite thick. Add the lemon juice and the prunes and allow them to heat through.

Adjust the seasoning and pour the sauce over the pork in the dish. Serve very hot.

Côtelettes De Porc Au Cidre *Pork Chops in Cider*

NORMANDY

A simple country dish, this uses the age-old combination of pork and apples. Although pork is not eaten a great deal in Normandy, when it is, it is almost always cooked with apples or with cider, if not both.

Preparation time: 10 minutes
Cooking time: 40 minutes
To serve: 6

6 pork chops, trimmed of excess fat
1 garlic clove, halved
salt
freshly ground black pepper
2 tablespoons butter or pork drippings
1 tablespoon flour
¾ cup cider
2 tablespoons water
1 fresh rosemary sprig
1 tablespoon crème fraîche (see page 118)
  or heavy cream

Rub the pork chops all over with the cut surface of the clove of garlic, then season generously on both sides with salt and pepper. Discard the garlic. Melt the butter or drippings in a deep skillet and quickly brown the chops on both sides. Remove and set aside.

Sprinkle the flour into the pan and stir well. Allow to brown. Gradually stir in the cider and bring to a boil, stirring well and scraping any sediment off the bottom of the pan. Add the water and simmer for 1 minute. Return the chops to the skillet with the rosemary, heat, cover and simmer for about 30 minutes or until the chops are cooked.

Stir the crème fraîche into the sauce and adjust the seasoning before serving.

Pieds De Porc St Ménéhould *Broiled Pig's Feet*

CHAMPAGNE

Pig's feet, cooked and bread crumbed, can often be seen in *charcuterie* windows in this part of northern France. The town of St Ménéhould prides itself on its specialty of feet that have been cooked for such a long time that they can be eaten, bones and all. It is almost impossible to achieve this degree of tenderness at home, but these crispy broiled feet make an excellent and economical hors d'oeuvre.

Preparation time: 20 minutes
Cooking time: $5\frac{1}{2}$ to $6\frac{1}{2}$ hours
Oven temperature: 425°
To serve: 6

6 pig's feet
2 onions, peeled
4 cloves
2 carrots, peeled
1 bouquet garni (2 bay leaves and large
    bunches of thyme, rosemary and parsley)
salt
$\frac{3}{4}$ cup wine vinegar
$\frac{1}{4}$ cup butter, softened
$1\frac{1}{2}$ cups fine dry white bread crumbs

Scrub and, if necessary, singe the feet. Either wrap them in a cheesecloth bag or tie them up well so that they do not lose their shape in the long slow cooking. Put them in a large saucepan together with the onions stuck with the cloves, the carrots, bouquet garni, some salt and the vinegar. Cover with plenty of cold water and bring to a boil. Cover the pan and simmer for 5 to 6 hours, by which time the feet should be very tender. Drain and leave until cool enough to be handled.

Brush each foot with the butter, then roll in the bread crumbs, pressing them in well. Lay in a shallow roasting pan and heat through for 15 minutes in the oven. Finish under a hot broiler so that the outside becomes very crisp and just short of charred.

Serve very hot, with mustard and dill pickles, or a vinaigrette or tartare sauce.

Côtes De Porc Savoyarde *Pork Chops with Cabbage and Cheese*

SAVOIE

This is an unusual, satisfying, all-in-one dish.

Preparation time: 20 minutes
Cooking time: 50 minutes to 1 hour
Oven temperature: 375°
To serve: 4

1 savoy cabbage, cored and shredded
5 tablespoons butter
1 onion, finely chopped
1 garlic clove, finely chopped
salt
freshly ground black pepper
4 juniper berries, crushed
4 pork chops
$1\frac{1}{4}$ cups white wine
1 tablespoon fine dry white bread crumbs
1 tablespoon grated Gruyère cheese

Blanch the cabbage in boiling salted water for 3 minutes. Drain well. Melt 2 tablespoons of the butter in a skillet, add the onion and garlic and fry until softened. Add the cabbage, season lightly with salt and pepper and stir in the juniper berries. Remove from the pan and set aside.

Season the chops on both sides with salt and pepper. Melt another 2 tablespoons of butter in the skillet and, when sizzling, quickly brown the chops on both sides.

Put half the cabbage mixture into an ovenproof serving dish, lay the pork chops on top, side by side, and cover with the remaining cabbage.

Pour the wine into the skillet and bring quickly to a boil, stirring to amalgamate any sediment left in the pan. Boil fiercely for 1 minute, then pour over the cabbage. Sprinkle on the bread crumbs mixed with the cheese, dot with the remaining butter and cook in the oven for 40 minutes, or until golden brown.

Chou Farci D'Auvergne *Stuffed Cabbage Casserole*

AUVERGNE

A good peasant dish to keep out the cold, this is not elegant, but very delicious. Gherkins may be served separately with this dish, and mustard is usually put on the table, too.

Preparation time: 30 minutes
Cooking time: 2½ hours
To serve: 6 to 8

1 large cabbage
3 onions, 1 whole and 2 finely chopped
2 garlic cloves, finely chopped
½ lb bulk sausage meat
¼ lb slab bacon, finely diced
4 slices of stale white bread, moistened with
    water and squeezed dry
1 tablespoon finely chopped fresh herbs –
    parsley, tarragon or chives
salt
freshly ground black pepper
2 eggs, beaten
1 lb piece of beef for pot-roasting
½ lb piece of boneless ham (uncooked or
    partially cooked)
2 leeks, chopped
1 bouquet garni
1 lb carrots, peeled
1½ lb potatoes, peeled

Peel off about 10 large outer leaves from the cabbage and plunge them into boiling salted water. Blanch for 5 minutes, then drain well. Mix the chopped onions and garlic into the sausage meat. Add the bacon, bread, herbs and salt and pepper to taste. Bind with the eggs.

Lay the cabbage leaves flat in a straight line, overlapping them closely. Spread the stuffing mixture along the center, then wrap the leaves right around to make a fat sausage shape. Tie up securely with string. Place in a large saucepan, together with the beef and the ham and cover with cold water. Bring very slowly to a boil, skimming off the scum that rises. Add the whole onion, leeks and bouquet garni, together with a little salt and pepper, bearing in mind that the ham may be quite salty. Simmer very gently for about 1½ hours.

Add the carrots and potatoes and continue to simmer for a further 30 minutes. Add the cabbage heart, quartered and cored, and continue to simmer until tender.

Lift out the pieces of meat and stuffed cabbage. Slice meat thickly and arrange on a heated serving platter. Surround with the carrots and potatoes, moisten with a little of the broth and serve very hot. (The remaining broth with its vegetables may be used to make a soup.)

Saucisses Aux Pommes *Pork Sausages Cooked with Apples*

ALSACE

A family dish, this uses the plump, highly seasoned pork sausages, bursting with coarsely chopped meat, in which this area excels. This method of cooking sausages with apples, which mellows the flavor, betrays the German influence on Alsatian cooking.

Preparation time: 15 minutes
Cooking time: 20 to 25 minutes
To serve: 6

6 large country pork sausage links
2 tablespoons butter
2 lb tart apples, peeled, cored and thinly
    sliced
salt
freshly ground black pepper

Prick the sausages in several places to prevent them from bursting. Melt the butter in a heavy deep skillet and add the sausages. Brown them quickly all over.

Add the apples to the pan, lower the heat, cover and cook over a gentle heat until the sausages are cooked. The apples should have reduced down to a savory purée.

Pâté De Pâques Berrichon *Berry Easter Pie*

BURGUNDY

This is the traditional Burgundy meat pie, which at Easter is made with hard-cooked eggs in the center and in a coffin shape. It can also be made as a round pie.

Preparation time: 40 minutes (plus
*   marinating and making pastry)*
Cooking time: 1½ hours
Oven temperature: 350°
To serve: 10 to 12

1 lb lean boneless pork, roughly chopped
1 lb lean boneless veal, roughly chopped
2 tablespoons brandy
¾ cup white wine
salt
freshly ground black pepper
pinch of ground allspice
pinch of grated nutmeg
pinch of cayenne
2 tablespoons finely chopped fresh parsley
1 quantity pâte brisée (see page 114)
4 hard-cooked eggs, shelled
2 bay leaves
1 small egg
1 tablespoon water

Put the meat in a bowl with the brandy, wine, salt and pepper and the spices. Leave to marinate in a cool place for a few hours.

Drain the meat and grind it coarsely. Moisten with the marinade, add the parsley and mix well. Fry a little pat of the mixture to taste for seasoning.

Roll out two-thirds of the dough to a rectangle about ¼ inch thick. Spread on half the meat mixture, leaving a 2 inch margin. Lay the hard-cooked eggs on top and cover with the remaining meat. Lay the bay leaves on top. Bring up the sides of the dough rectangle to make flat, perpendicular sides, and form triangle shaped ends to resemble a coffin.

Roll out the remaining dough to form a lid, and pinch the moistened edges together to seal well. Decorate with dough leaves and cut a vent in the top.

Place on a baking sheet and brush all over with the egg lightly beaten with the water. Bake in the oven.

Serve cold, or just slightly warm.

Côtes de porc Savoyarde (page 81), chou farci d'Auvergne and
escalopes de veau Chambery (page 85)

Baeckenhofe *Lamb, Pork and Beef Baked with Potatoes*

ALSACE

This northern cousin of the better-known cassoulet of the south is the perfect dish for cold weather. As it needs such long slow cooking (it used to be carried to the baker's, and left in his oven overnight), it is only worth making in large quantities, but it reheats well, so you can make two meals at one time.

Preparation time: 30 minutes (plus
*   marinating overnight)*
Cooking time: 4 hours minimum
Oven temperature: 300°
To serve: 10 to 12

1 lb pork for stew, cut into cubes
1 lb lamb for stew, cut into cubes
1 lb beef for stew, cut into cubes
1 lb onions, 1 whole and the rest thinly
*   sliced into rings*
4 cloves
2 garlic cloves, peeled
1 bouquet garni
2 cups white wine
salt
freshly ground black pepper
butter
2 lb potatoes, peeled and thinly sliced

Put all the meat into a large bowl, add the whole onion stuck with the cloves, the garlic cloves, the bouquet garni, wine and plenty of salt and pepper and leave to marinate overnight.

The next day butter a large casserole, preferably earthenware. Put in a layer of potatoes, and sprinkle with a little salt and pepper. Add a layer of the drained meat and cover with a layer of sliced onions. Repeat, ending with a layer of potatoes. Pour on the strained marinade.

Cover the casserole and seal the lid with a little flour and water paste. Cook in the oven for at least 4 hours. Serve straight from the oven and break the seal at the table, so that everyone can enjoy the full aroma.

Choucroûte Alsacienne *Braised Sauerkraut with Pork*

ALSACE

A hearty dish for hearty eaters, this is not worth making in small quantities, especially as it is every bit as good reheated. The exact proportion of meat and sausages is not important and will depend on what is available at your local supermarket, but all the meat must be pork-based.

Preparation time: 30 minutes
Cooking time: 2½ hours
Oven temperature: 350°
To serve: 10 to 12

¼ *cup pork, duck or goose fat*
4 *lb sauerkraut, rinsed and drained*
4 *onions, peeled*
8 *cloves*
3 *carrots, peeled*
2 *tart apples, peeled, cored and chopped*
freshly ground black pepper
12 *juniper berries*
1 *lb piece of Canadian bacon*
1 *ham hock*
2 *cups white wine*
1 *large garlicky salami*
10 *hot Italian sausage links*
10 *frankfurters or kielbasi*

Melt the fat in a large flameproof casserole, add the sauerkraut, the onions stuck with the cloves, the carrots and apples. Sprinkle over pepper to taste and the juniper berries, then bury the piece of Canadian bacon and the ham hock in the center. Add the wine and enough water just to come to the top of the sauerkraut. Cover and simmer on top of the stove or in the oven for 1 hour.

Add the salami and Italian sausages, bury them also in the middle of the sauerkraut mixture and continue to cook for another hour. Top up with a little water from time to time if necessary to prevent the choucroûte from sticking on the bottom.

Add the frankfurters and cook for a further 30 minutes.

To serve, discard the onions and carrots and pile the sauerkraut in the center of a large heated serving dish. Slice the Canadian bacon and ham into thick pieces and lay these down the center of the dish. Surround with the sausages.

Escalopes De Veau Chambéry *Veal Cutlets with Vermouth*

SAVOIE

Chambéry, once the seat of the Dukes of Savoy, is a picturesque city and the home of the excellent dry vermouth that bears its name and that gives this dish its subtle flavor.

Preparation time: 5 minutes
Cooking time: 15 minutes
To serve: 4

4 *veal cutlets*
salt
freshly ground black pepper
lemon juice
¼ *cup butter*
5 *tablespoons dry vermouth*
¾ *cup crème fraîche (see page 118)*

Season the cutlets liberally on both sides with salt, pepper and lemon juice. Melt the butter in a heavy skillet and when foaming add the cutlets. Fry them quickly until just golden brown on both sides. Remove from the pan and keep hot.

Add the vermouth to the skillet and stir well to loosen any sediment. Bring quickly to a boil and boil for 1 minute to reduce. Add the crème fraîche and stir until smooth. Bring just to a boil.

Adjust the seasoning, then return the cutlets to the pan and simmer for 1 minute to allow the meat to heat through and the sauce to thicken a little. Serve very hot.

Escalopes De Veau Au Calvados *Veal Cutlets with Apple Brandy*

NORMANDY

This is a dish for special occasions which is very quick to make.

Preparation time: 10 minutes
Cooking time: 10 to 15 minutes
To serve: 6

6 veal cutlets
salt
freshly ground black pepper
¼ cup butter
1 cup thinly sliced button mushrooms
3 tablespoons Calvados or brandy
¾ cup crème fraîche (see page 118) or
    heavy cream

Beat the veal cutlets between two sheets of wax paper using a meat mallet or rolling pin until they are very thin. Season well with salt and pepper on both sides. Melt the butter in a deep skillet and sear the cutlets quickly on both sides. Remove from the pan and keep warm.

Add the mushrooms to the skillet and cook for 3 minutes or until soft. Return the veal to the pan and heat through. Warm the Calvados or brandy, set it alight and pour into the skillet. When the flames have died down, stir in the crème fraîche or cream and adjust the seasoning. Bring just to a boil and serve.

Côtes De Veau A La Comtoise *Veal Chops with Cheese*

FRANCHE-COMTE

The smoked ham of the Franche-Comté has a robust flavor, and together with the local Comté cheese gives the veal in this dish a quite unusual "bite."

Preparation time: 5 minutes
Cooking time: 15 minutes
To serve: 6

6 veal chops
salt
freshly ground black pepper
3 tablespoons butter
1 tablespoon oil
6 slices of smoked ham
6 slices of Comté or Gruyère cheese
¾ cup white wine

Season the chops well on both sides with salt and pepper. Melt 2 tablespoons of the butter with the oil in a heavy skillet and quickly brown the chops on each side. Transfer the chops to a flat baking dish. Lay a piece of ham on top of each one and top with a slice of cheese.

Place under a hot broiler or in a hot oven and cook for 5 minutes, or until the cheese has melted, is bubbling and just beginning to brown.

Pour the wine into the skillet, bring to a boil and allow to bubble for 1 minute, stirring to amalgamate any sediment. Add the remaining butter cut into small pieces to give the sauce a glaze and pour over the chops. Serve very hot.

Côtes de veau à la Comtoise, saucisses aux pommes (page 82)
and rognons de porc flambé (page 93)

Blanquette De Veau A L'Ancienne

Veal Stew with Onions, Mushrooms and Cream

SAVOIE

This delicious, comforting dish, like most stews, is probably best made a day or two ahead and left to mature. If this is done, however, the last step – the addition of cream and egg yolks – should be left until the veal is to be reheated and served. The light flavor of the meat is an essential quality, so it is necessary to buy the palest, freshest young veal. The usual accompaniment is noodles or boiled potatoes.

Preparation time: 30 minutes
Cooking time: 2 hours
To serve: 6

3 lb boneless veal shoulder, cut into 2 inch
  chunks
1 large onion, studded with 2 cloves
2 carrots, quartered
1 celery stalk, cut in half
1 leek, cut in half
bouquet garni
salt
freshly ground black pepper
1 quart homemade chicken stock or canned
  chicken broth
18–20 pearl onions, peeled
¼ cup butter
¼ cup flour
1 lb small button mushrooms
1 teaspoon lemon juice
3 egg yolks
¾ cup light cream
chopped fresh parsley to garnish

Place the veal in a flameproof casserole. Cover with cold water, bring to a boil and blanch for 2 to 3 minutes. Drain and rinse under cold water to remove all traces of scum. Return the veal to the clean casserole.

Place the onion, carrots, celery, leek and bouquet garni on top of the meat. Season and cover with the chicken stock. If any of the meat or vegetables are still exposed, add water. Bring to a boil once again and skim off any scum. Reduce the heat and simmer the veal, partially covered, for 1½ hours or until tender but not overcooked.

Meanwhile, place the pearl onions in a saucepan, together with some of the stock from the simmering casserole, and bring to a boil. Cover, reduce the heat and simmer for 20 minutes, or until the onions are tender. Remove the onions with a slotted spoon and put aside. Pour the liquid into the simmering veal.

When the veal is tender, pour the contents of the saucepan into a colander over a bowl. Melt the butter in a saucepan and add the flour. Cook for 2 minutes, stirring continuously. Ladle in 1 quart of the veal stock, stirring as the sauce thickens. Add the mushrooms and lemon juice and gently fold into the sauce. Cook for about 5 minutes then add the veal and the reserved onions to the sauce and mushrooms.

Beat the egg yolks and cream in a bowl until thoroughly combined. Stir into the veal. Heat again briefly, to thicken the sauce, but do not allow to boil.

Spoon the blanquette into the center of a heated serving plate and arrange cooked noodles or potatoes around the edge. Garnish with the parsley, and serve.

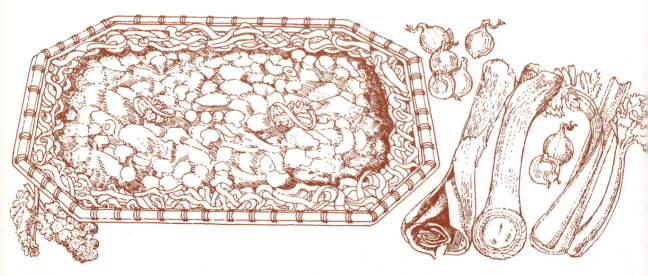

Cassoulet De Toulouse

Casserole of Beans with Pork and Lamb

LANGUEDOC

Three towns in the Languedoc – Castel-naudry, Toulouse and Carcassone – claim this classic dish as their own. Each has its own particular variation, but the basic ingredients of the cassoulet are dried white beans, a well-flavored pork sausage, and a piece of preserved goose (*confit d'oie*). The latter can be bought canned, but if it is not available a perfectly good *cassoulet* can be made without it. This version, from Toulouse, which includes lamb as well as pork, is particularly satisfying.

Essential is a really large cassoulet pot, or casserole.

Preparation time: 1 hour
Cooking time: about 3 hours
Oven temperature: 300°
To serve: 10 to 12

2 lb dried white navy beans
2 tablespoons oil or fat from preserved goose
2 onions, thinly sliced
3 garlic cloves, finely chopped
½ lb piece of salt pork or slab bacon
1 lb loin or shoulder of pork, boned
1 small shoulder of lamb (or ½ large one), boned
1 piece preserved goose (optional)
1 lb piece coarse pork and garlic salami
¼ cup tomato paste
7 cups water
salt
freshly ground black pepper
1 bouquet garni
2 cups soft bread crumbs (see method)

Rinse the beans in cold water, then put into a large saucepan. Cover with cold water, bring slowly to a boil and simmer for 5 minutes. Remove from the heat, cover and leave to soak in the water while you prepare the remaining ingredients.

Heat the oil or goose fat in a large skillet and fry the onions and garlic until softened. Raise the heat and brown on all sides, in turn, the salt pork or bacon, the pork, the shoulder of lamb, the piece of goose and the salami. Remove each from the skillet when it is browned and set aside. Add the tomato paste to the pan with a little of the water, stir well to amalgamate any sediment and bring quickly to a boil.

Drain the beans, rinse them and put them in a clean saucepan with the remaining cold water. Bring to a boil, then pour the beans and water into the cassoulet pot. Add the contents of the skillet, salt and pepper to taste and stir well. Bury the salt pork or bacon, the pork, the shoulder of lamb, the preserved goose and the salami in the beans, add the bouquet garni, and bring to simmering point on top of the stove.

Sprinkle on a thick layer of bread crumbs and place the cassoulet pot in the oven. Cook for 2 to 3 hours. From time to time press down the crust which will have formed on top and sprinkle on a further layer of bread crumbs. Tradition has it that the crust must be pressed down and renewed seven times, but after three times you should have a lovely golden crust. Larger pieces of meat should be cut up before serving.

Truffade *Potato, Bacon and Cheese Pancake*

AUVERGNE

This recipe is found with variations all over the area of the *massif central*, using whichever is the local cheese, which might be a Tomme, a Beaufort, a Gruyère or a Cantal. Serve these potato pancakes on their own as a light supper dish, or to accompany a robust meat dish.

Preparation time: 20 minutes
Cooking time: about 15 minutes
To serve: 4

$\frac{1}{2}$ *lb cheese (see above), diced*
1 lb potatoes, peeled and sliced wafer-thin
salt
freshly ground black pepper
$\frac{1}{4}$ *lb slab bacon, diced*
2 tablespoons lard

Make in two or four batches, using half or a quarter of the ingredients for each batch.

Mingle the cheese gently with the potatoes and season the mixture with salt and pepper. Melt the bacon in a skillet over a low heat until the fat begins to run. Add the lard to the skillet, raise the heat and when the fat begins to smoke, add the potato mixture to the pan. Lower the heat and cook, stirring, for 5 minutes, then leave to cook over a moderate heat until the bottom of the pancake is crisp and brown. Invert onto heated plates to serve.

Ris De Veau A La Crème *Veal Sweetbreads in Cream*

BRITTANY

Variety meats are one of the mainstays of French cuisine, and sweetbreads are among the most delicate and prized items of the repertoire. Veal sweetbreads are the best, although lamb sweetbreads can also be used. The soaking, blanching and pressing can be done a day ahead of time, leaving the actual cooking to take no longer than the average supper dish. Some butchers sell their sweetbreads already prepared, so ask when you buy.

These sweetbreads are particularly delicious served in a warm patty shell or pastry case.

Preparation time: 1 hour (plus soaking and
*   pressing)*
Cooking time: 45 minutes
Oven temperature: 325°
To serve: 4

1 lb veal sweetbreads
4 bacon slices
1 large onion, sliced
2 carrots, sliced
$\frac{3}{4}$ *cup chicken broth*
$\frac{3}{4}$ *cup white wine*
$\frac{1}{4}$ *cup butter (optional)*
$\frac{3}{4}$ *cup heavy cream*
2 teaspoons chopped fresh parsley
salt
freshly ground black pepper

If the sweetbreads have not been prepared, soak them in cold water until they turn white. This usually requires about 3 hours, and the water should be changed three or four times to remove impurities. When the sweetbreads are clean, fill a saucepan with cold salted water, add the sweetbreads and bring to a boil, stirring constantly but gently to agitate the sweetbreads and continue the clearing process. When the water begins to boil, remove the sweetbreads and drain them thoroughly. Their consistency is now much tougher, and they can be handled and trimmed.

After trimming, put the sweetbreads on paper towels, on either a board or plate, and cover with a heavy weight. Press the sweetbreads for at least 1 hour, or overnight.

Wrap each pressed sweetbread with a slice of bacon. Place the onion and carrots on the bottom of a flameproof casserole. Lay the sweetbreads on top of the vegetables and pour over the broth and wine. Scatter over the parsley. Bring to a boil gently, then remove from the heat, cover and cook in the oven for about 45 minutes.

When the sweetbreads are tender, remove with a slotted spoon and place on a heated serving dish. Alternatively, they may be browned very gently in the butter over a low heat, while the sauce is being made. Bring the cooking liquid to a boil and boil briskly to reduce by half. Turn down the heat, stir in the cream and parsley and add salt and pepper to taste. Strain the sauce over the sweetbreads, and serve.

Foie de veau à la Lyonnaise and truffade

Foie De Veau A La Lyonnaise *Calf's Liver with Onions*

LYONNAIS

Onions are one of the hallmarks of Lyonnaise cooking, and this is a delicious way of preparing liver.

Preparation time: 15 minutes
Cooking time: 10 minutes
To serve: 4

1 lb calf's liver
1 tablespoon flour
½ cup butter
1 lb onions, thinly sliced
salt
freshly ground black pepper
1 tablespoon wine vinegar

Cut the liver into thick slices, diagonally, and dredge each slice lightly with flour. Melt half the butter in a skillet. When it is foaming and just beginning to darken, add the liver and brown quickly on both sides. Remove to a heated serving dish and keep hot.

Add the remaining butter to the skillet, heat and add the onions. Cook over a high heat until they brown, stirring so that they brown evenly. Season to taste with salt and pepper, then add the vinegar and bring quickly to a boil.

Pile the onion mixture over the liver and serve very hot.

Rognons D'Agneau Au Champagne _Lamb Kidneys Cooked in Champagne_

CHAMPAGNE

The Champagne that would be used for this delicate and luxurious dish, which can of course also be made with veal kidneys, would be the still Champagne, or _Champagne nature_ of the region, which unfortunately can only be drunk locally as it is not thought to export well. Any other good dry white wine may be used instead. Serve with a simple green salad.

Preparation time: 15 minutes
Cooking time: 20 minutes
To serve: 6

$\frac{1}{2}$ cup butter
12 lamb kidneys, skinned, cored and thickly
  sliced
6 to 8 shallots, finely chopped
2 cups thinly sliced mushrooms
1 tablespoon flour
$\frac{3}{4}$ cup still Champagne or white wine
salt
freshly ground black pepper
2 tablespoons crème fraîche (see page 118)
  or heavy cream
squeeze of lemon juice

Melt half the butter in a heavy-based skillet, add the kidneys and cook until they change color.

Meanwhile melt the remaining butter in a small heavy saucepan and cook the shallots until they are soft and golden. Add the mushrooms, raise the heat and cook quickly for 2 minutes. Remove from the heat and keep warm.

Sprinkle the kidneys with the flour, stir well and cook without browning for 2 minutes. Stir in the wine to make a smooth sauce and incorporate any sediment on the bottom of the pan. Cover and simmer for 5 minutes or until the kidneys are cooked.

Stir in the mushroom and shallot mixture and salt and pepper to taste, then add the cream and lemon juice. Bring quickly to a boil and serve very hot.

Rognons De Veau Au Chablis _Veal Kidneys Cooked in Chablis_

BURGUNDY

The subtle but full flavor of a Chablis wine blends beautifully with the delicate taste and texture of veal kidneys. If these are not available, you can make the dish with lamb kidneys, but it will not be quite so delicate. Serve with plain boiled rice.

Preparation time: 20 minutes
Cooking time: 20 minutes
To serve: 4

4 veal kidneys, sliced
1 tablespoon oil
salt
freshly ground black pepper
pinch of dried thyme
1 bay leaf, crumbled
$\frac{1}{4}$ cup butter
1 tablespoon finely chopped shallots
$\frac{1}{4}$ bottle of Chablis
juice of $\frac{1}{2}$ lemon (or less, according to taste)
$\frac{1}{2}$ tablespoon finely chopped fresh parsley

Sprinkle the kidneys with the oil, salt and pepper and the herbs and leave for at least 10 minutes.

Melt half the butter in a skillet, add the kidney slices and fry quickly until they have changed color. Turn into a heated serving dish and keep hot.

Add the shallots to the skillet and sweat until they soften. Add the wine, bring to a boil and boil for a few minutes to reduce, stirring well to loosen any sediment on the bottom of the pan.

Add the lemon juice and salt and pepper to taste, then stir in the remaining butter, cut into small pieces, to give the sauce a glaze. Pour the sauce over the kidneys, sprinkle with the parsley and serve very hot.

Tripe A La Mode De Caen *Tripe in the Caen Manner*

NORMANDY

This famous dish can often be bought cooked and ready to serve in Normandy and large cities in France. It is usually of excellent quality because it is made in large quantities by first class specialists. However, although its preparation is long, it is easy to make.

Preparation time: 15 minutes
Cooking time: 6 hours
Oven temperature: 300°
To serve: 6

2 lb partially cooked fresh tripe
1–2 cow heels or calves' feet
salt
freshly ground black pepper
2 bay leaves
2 sprigs of parsley
4 large onions, peeled
4 cloves
4 leeks, sliced
2 carrots, sliced
2½ cups cider or dry white wine
¼ cup Calvados (optional)

Wash the tripe very thoroughly and blanch it, then cut into small pieces. Divide up the cow heels. Place in a heavy casserole with the tripe, seasoning, herbs, the onions (each with a clove stuck in it) and the sliced leeks and carrots. Add the cider or wine and the Calvados (if used). Cover and cook in the oven for 6 hours.

This dish may be left overnight. Remove the fat from the surface and take out the cow heel bones and the herbs before reheating for serving.

Rognons De Porc Flambés *Kidneys Flambé*

LORRAINE

A very simple, quick and economical dish, this is delicious enough for a special occasion. Serve with rice or noodles, followed by a simple green salad.

Preparation time: 10 minutes
Cooking time: 10 to 15 minutes
To serve: 4

6 tablespoons butter
8 shallots, finely chopped
4 pork kidneys, skinned, cored and sliced
2 tablespoons brandy
pinch of cayenne
pinch of dried thyme
salt
freshly ground black pepper
½ cup white wine
1 tablespoon finely chopped fresh parsley

Melt ¼ cup of the butter in a heavy skillet, add the shallots and fry until softened. Add the kidneys and cook over a fairly high heat for 3 minutes, stirring.

When the kidneys have all changed color, add the brandy and set alight. Take off the heat and wait for the flames to die down.

Add the cayenne, thyme and salt and pepper to taste. Return to a moderate heat and cook for 2 to 3 minutes, until the kidneys are cooked. Add the wine, stir well to amalgamate, bring to a boil and let the sauce bubble for 2 minutes. Add the remaining butter, cut into small pieces, to give the sauce a glaze. Sprinkle with the parsley and serve very hot.

Lièvre Angoumois

Hare in Wine and Currant Jelly
GUYENNE

This dish is named after the town and region of Angouleme, a rich area bounded on the left by the cognac distilleries of the Charente and on the right by the truffles and walnuts of the Perigord. It is fairly hilly country, abundant with all kinds of game. Numerous soft fruits – including currants, grapes and cherries – are commercial products of the Angoumois, and this recipe combines the cultivated bounty with that of the wild.

Preparation time: 15 minutes
Cooking time: 4 hours
Oven temperature: 325°
To serve: 6

1 hare, skinned, dressed and cut up
2 tablespoons lard
4 slices of bacon, chopped
1 onion, stuck with 2 cloves
1 carrot, sliced
1 celery stalk, sliced
1 quart beef broth
bouquet garni
juice of $\frac{1}{2}$ lemon
3 tablespoons flour
1 teaspoon currant jelly
$\frac{1}{2}$ cup red wine

Place the pieces of the hare in a large flameproof casserole, together with the lard and bacon. Sauté the hare over a medium heat for about 5 minutes or until lightly browned. Add the vegetables and enough broth to cover the hare. Add the bouquet garni and lemon juice. Bring to a boil, then cover and cook in the oven for 4 hours, checking occasionally to make sure that there is enough liquid in the pot. Remove the onion.

Just before serving, skim any fat from the casserole. Blend the flour with a little cold water until smooth, then stir slowly into the casserole. Add the jelly and wine and simmer, uncovered, for a few minutes until the sauce has reduced and thickened.

Râble De Lièvre A La Crème

LORRAINE

This method of cooking hare, which shows the influence of German cuisine in this region, mellows the strong flavor of the hare, and makes it into a rich and velvety delicacy.

Preparation time: 15 minutes (plus 3 hours minimum marinating)
Cooking time: 50 minutes
Oven temperature: 375°
To serve: 4 to 6

1 saddle of hare, including the hind legs, skinned
1 tablespoon oil
1 teaspoon wine vinegar
salt
freshly ground black pepper
1 thyme branch
1 rosemary branch
$\frac{1}{4}$ cup butter
$\frac{3}{4}$ cup crème fraîche (see page 118) or heavy cream

Faisan à la vigneronne (page 60),
râble de lièvre à la piron and
lapin à la moutarde (page 96)

Saddle of Hare with Cream

Lay the hare in a roasting pan, dribble on the oil and the vinegar, sprinkle with salt and pepper and lay the thyme and rosemary on top. Leave to marinate for several hours, turning the hare over occasionally.

When ready to cook, remove thyme and rosemary, melt the butter and when sizzling, pour over the hare. Place in the oven and cook for 40 minutes, basting and turning the hare over several times. Take great care not to let the sediment at the bottom of the pan burn, as this will give a very bitter taste; if necessary add a little more oil.

Remove the hare – the meat should be just pink inside – carve into thick slices and keep warm on a heated serving dish.

Add the cream to the juices in the roasting pan and bring quickly to a boil, scraping up any sediment on the bottom of the pan. Boil until the sauce thickens Season to taste with salt and pepper, adding a few drops more wine vinegar if necessary, and serve very hot.

Râble De Lièvre A La Piron

Marinated Saddle of Hare with Grapes
BURGUNDY

This is one of the great classics of Burgundian cooking, traditionally eaten to celebrate the end of the grape harvest. Extravagant though it is, it is a beautiful dish, well worth making for a special occasion.

Preparation time: 30 minutes plus 2 to 3
   days marinating
Cooking time: 25 to 30 minutes
Oven temperature: 375°
To serve: 4 to 6

$\frac{1}{4}$ lb pork fat, cut into larding strips
1 saddle of hare, skinned
4 shallots, roughly chopped
1 garlic clove, roughly chopped
1 fresh thyme branch
2 bay leaves, crumbled
1 celery stalk, roughly chopped
salt
freshly ground black pepper
1 cup brandy
$\frac{1}{2}$ cup butter, melted
1 tablespoon wine vinegar
2 tablespoons heavy cream
1 cup seedless grapes, peeled
1 cup purple grapes, peeled and seeded

Thread the pork fat strips into the flesh of the hare at intervals, using a larding needle. Put into a bowl, add the shallots, garlic, herbs, celery and salt and pepper and pour over $\frac{3}{4}$ cup of the brandy. Leave in a cool place to marinate for 2 to 3 days, turning the hare frequently.

Drain the hare, reserving the marinade, and place in a roasting pan. Sprinkle with a little more salt and pepper, pour on the melted butter and roast in the oven until just cooked – the inside must remain pink.

Remove the hare to a heated serving dish. Warm the remaining brandy, pour over the hare and set alight. Leave until the flames die down.

Pour the strained marinade into the roasting pan, add the vinegar and bring quickly to a boil. Add the cream and stir until smooth. Adjust the seasoning. Pour the sauce over the hare, surround with the grapes and serve.

Lapin A La Moutarde *Rabbit Cooked with Mustard*

BURGUNDY

Stuffed, and covered with the local Dijon mustard, this rabbit dish is a highly tasty specialty of the area.

Preparation time: 30 minutes
Cooking time: about 1 hour
Oven temperature: 375°
To serve: 4 to 6

1 rabbit, skinned and dressed
1 tablespoon brandy
¼ cup butter
1 onion, finely chopped
4 shallots, finely chopped
2 garlic cloves, finely chopped
1 rabbit liver, finely chopped
¼ lb chicken livers, finely chopped
4 slices of stale white bread
¾ cup milk
½ tablespoon finely chopped fresh parsley
½ teaspoon dried thyme
1 bay leaf, crumbled
salt
freshly ground black pepper
1 egg, beaten
3 tablespoons Dijon-style mustard
2 tablespoons fine dry white bread crumbs
¾ cup crème fraîche (see page 118)

Rub the rabbit inside and out with the brandy.

Melt half the butter in a skillet, add the onion, shallots and garlic and fry until softened. Take the pan off the heat and gently mix in the chopped rabbit and chicken livers.

Soak the bread briefly in the milk, squeeze out and place in a mixing bowl. Add the onion and liver mixture, the parsley, thyme and bay leaf, season generously with salt and pepper and bind together with the egg. Stuff the rabbit with this mixture and place in a roasting pan.

Spread the mustard all over the rabbit and sprinkle with the breadcrumbs, patting them in firmly. Dot with the remaining butter and roast in the oven, basting from time to time and adding a little more butter if necessary. When the rabbit is cooked, remove it to a heated serving platter. Keep hot.

Add the cream to the juices in the roasting pan, stir well and add a little water if necessary to remove all the sediment from the bottom of the pan. Bring quickly to a boil, adjust the seasoning and pour over the rabbit before serving.

Côtelettes De Chevreuil d'Uzes *Venison Chops Uzes Style*

LANGUEDOC

Chevreuil is the young roebuck of the area, which is very tender and can take quick cooking. Older meat may need marinating overnight in a mixture of olive oil and white wine.

Preparation time: 10 minutes
Cooking time: 20 minutes
Serves: 4

4 venison chops
2 tablespoons oil
¼ cup butter
4 slices of bread, cut into heart shapes
5 tablespoons wine vinegar
1 cup beef broth
1¼ cups light cream
1 orange, the rind cut into thin strips and a
    little juice
2 tablespoons blanched almonds
4 small gherkins, cut into thin strips
freshly ground black pepper

Sauté the chops on both sides in the oil. Arrange them in a warm serving dish in the shape of an overlapping circle and keep warm. Add the butter to the pan in which the chops were cooked and fry the bread. Arrange the croûtons alternately with the chops. Scrape the bottom of the pan and stir in the vinegar to lift the sediment. Add the broth and cream. Bring to a boil and reduce to thicken slightly.

Strain the sauce and return to a clean pan. Add the strips of orange rind, a little juice, the almonds and gherkins and season with black pepper. Reheat the sauce and pour over the chops to serve.

Vegetables

Gratin Dauphinois *Gratiné Potatoes Baked in Cream*

DAUPHINE

An utterly creamy, melting-in-the-mouth potato dish, which is good enough to be eaten on its own but also enhances dishes of chicken or veal or baked fish.

Preparation time: 30 minutes
Cooking time: 2 hours
Oven temperature: 375°
To serve: 4 to 6

2 lb potatoes, peeled and very thinly sliced
1 garlic clove, halved
¼ cup butter
salt
freshly ground black pepper
2 cups heavy cream

Soak the potatoes in cold water for at least 10 minutes to extract some of the starch, then drain and pat them dry.

Rub a large shallow gratin dish with the cut surface of the clove of garlic, then butter it generously, using 1 tablespoon of the butter. Arrange a layer of potato slices in the bottom of the dish, sprinkle with salt and pepper, and dot with small pieces of butter. Continue until all the potatoes have been used.

Bring the cream just to a boil in a saucepan. Pour over the potatoes and dot with the remaining butter. Bake in the oven until the potatoes have absorbed all the cream and are very tender. If the potatoes seem to be drying out too quickly, cover with a sheet of foil.

When ready, the top should be golden brown.

Gratin Savoyard *Gratiné Potatoes*

SAVOIE

This is the simplest of the potato gratins, which are among the best loved specialties of this mountainous, central district of France. It makes a particularly good accompaniment to beef or game.

Preparation time: 30 minutes
Cooking time: 1 to 1½ hours
Oven temperature: 400°
To serve: 4 to 6

2 lb potatoes, peeled and very thinly sliced
2 garlic cloves, 1 halved and 1 very finely
    chopped
¼ cup butter
salt
freshly ground black pepper
1 cup shredded Gruyère or Comté cheese
1¼ cups boiling beef broth

Soak the potatoes in cold water for at least 10 minutes to extract some of the starch, then drain and pat them dry.

Rub a large shallow gratin dish with the cut surface of the halved clove of garlic, then butter the dish very generously, using nearly half the butter. Arrange a layer of potato slices on the bottom of the dish and sprinkle with salt and pepper, a little chopped garlic and some grated cheese. Repeat until all the potatoes have been used, but keep aside a good 2 tablespoons of the cheese. Pour on the hot broth.

Finish with a thick sprinkling of cheese and dot with the remaining butter. Cook in the oven until the potatoes have absorbed all the liquid and are tender, and the top is golden brown and crisp.

If the potatoes are cooked but the top not browned, raise the oven heat for the last 10 minutes, or brown under the broiler.

Gratin Dauphinoise and gratin Savoyarde

Carottes Vichy *Cooked Carrots*

BOURBONNAIS

Carrots are used a great deal in the cooking of this part of central France. Vichy water, which is particularly soft, may be used locally, but ordinary tap water will also do perfectly well for this way of cooking carrots. It is one of the simplest and best in bringing out their flavor.

Young carrots may be left whole; older ones should be cut into thick slices.

Preparation time: 10 minutes
Cooking time: 15 to 20 minutes
To serve: 4

1 lb carrots, whole or sliced (see above)
¾ cup water
2 tablespoons butter
1 sugar cube
salt
freshly ground black pepper
1 tablespoon finely chopped fresh parsley

Put the carrots into a heavy saucepan with the water, half the butter, the sugar and salt and pepper and simmer until the carrots are just tender and all the water has evaporated. Watch that they do not boil dry and add a little more water if necessary.

Add the remaining butter and swirl around the pan to melt it and coat the carrots. Sprinkle with the parsley before serving.

Carottes A La Nivernaise *Glazed Carrots and Onions*

NIVERNAIS

One of the classic ways of garnishing a meat dish, these glazed carrots and small onions are equally delicious with beef, veal or lamb, or eaten alone as a vegetable side dish. Use small young carrots whole; cut older ones into thick slices. Use small pearl onions, or, if possible, the small flat French onions.

Preparation time: 20 minutes
Cooking time: 20 to 30 minutes
To serve: 4 to 6

½ lb carrots, whole or thickly sliced (see above)
½ lb pearl onions, peeled
1 cup water
2 tablespoons butter
1 sugar cube
salt
freshly ground black pepper
2 tablespoons meat stock or juice from a roast
1 teaspoon sugar

Put the carrots and onions into a heavy saucepan with the water, half the butter, the sugar cube and salt and pepper and simmer until all the water has evaporated and the vegetables are just tender.

Add the meat stock, sugar and the remaining butter, raise the heat a little and cook until just beginning to brown slightly.

Adjust the seasoning before serving.

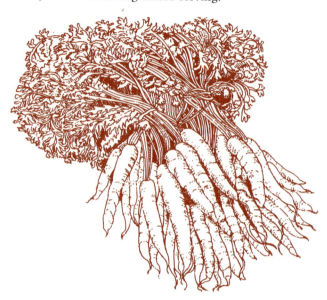

Petits Pois A La Nivernaise *Peas with Carrots and Onions*

NIVERNAIS

A delicious and very pretty mixture of fresh young vegetables, this should really be eaten on its own, after the main dish.

Preparation time: 30 minutes
Cooking time: 30 minutes
To serve: 6

¼ cup butter
2 bunches of young carrots, scrubbed or scraped
½ lb pearl onions, peeled
1 small head of lettuce, leaves separated
1 lb (about 2 cups) shelled peas
salt
freshly ground black pepper
pinch of sugar
¾ cup water
2 tablespoons crème fraîche (see page 118) or heavy cream

Melt the butter in a large, heavy saucepan, add the carrots, onions and lettuce leaves and turn well so that they become evenly coated with butter. Cover and sweat very gently for 5 minutes.

Add the peas, salt and pepper, the sugar and water, cover again and simmer gently until the peas are just tender. All the vegetables should be cooked through, but not too soft.

Stir in the cream, adjust the seasoning and serve with the cooking liquid.

100

Les Navets Au Sucre *Turnips with Sugar*

MAINE

Root vegetables grow well in this northern part of France, and are eaten a great deal, especially in the country. They are always eaten young, and usually served on their own, so that their full flavor, brought out in the cooking, can be properly appreciated.

Preparation time: 10 minutes
Cooking time: 15 to 25 minutes
To serve: 4

2 tablespoons butter
2 tablespoons sugar
1 lb young turnips, peeled
$\frac{1}{4}$ cup water or broth
salt
freshly ground black pepper
1 tablespoon finely chopped fresh parsley

Melt the butter and sugar together in a saucepan over a low heat. Add the whole turnips and cook gently for 5 minutes, turning them so that they become evenly coated with the butter and sugar. Add the water or broth and salt and pepper to taste, then cover and simmer until the turnips are tender, shaking the pan from time to time.

Adjust the seasoning and sprinkle with the parsley before serving.

Marrons Braisés *Braised Chestnuts*

GUYENNE

Inland, throughout the southwestern corner of France, the roads are lined with chestnut trees. Chestnuts are used not only to make the famous marrons glacés and other sweet dishes, but also in savory cooking, to accompany meat dishes, especially game, or to add body to stuffings or to other vegetables.

Braised as here they make an excellent accompaniment to turkey, venison or other game, and they are also sometimes eaten quite plain in the Limousin, boiled and peeled, with salt, pepper and a little butter. The easiest way to peel chestnuts is to put them into a large saucepan, cover with cold water, bring to a boil and boil for 2 minutes. Take them out a few at a time, keeping the others hot, and peel as soon as they are cool enough to handle. If towards the end the chestnuts become difficult to peel, bring briefly to a boil again.

Preparation time: 2 minutes (plus peeling
  chestnuts)
Cooking time: 40 to 50 minutes
To serve: 4 to 6

1 lb chestnuts, peeled
2 tablespoons butter
1$\frac{1}{4}$ cups broth
salt
freshly ground black pepper

Put all the ingredients into a heavy saucepan, cover and bring to a boil. Simmer for 40 to 50 minutes or until the chestnuts are tender without having disintegrated, and all the liquid has been absorbed. If necessary, leave the lid off the pan for the last 15 minutes cooking, to allow excess moisture to evaporate.

Adjust the seasoning before serving.

Pipérade *Ragoût of Peppers and Tomatoes*

LANGUEDOC

A simple dish, from the Basque country, this can be served as an appetizer or as a light main dish.

Preparation time: 15 minutes
Cooking time: 30 minutes
To serve: 4 to 6

2 tablespoons olive oil or goose or pork
  drippings
2 large onions, thinly sliced
1 garlic clove, finely chopped (optional)
1 lb sweet peppers, cored, seeded and cut into
  strips
1 lb tomatoes, peeled and roughly chopped
6 eggs
1 teaspoon finely chopped fresh parsley or
  basil
salt
freshly ground black pepper
triangles of fried bread to garnish

Heat the oil or drippings in a deep skillet or shallow flame-proof casserole, add the onions and garlic and fry gently until golden yellow. Add the peppers and cook for 10 to 15 minutes, or until they are soft. Stir in the tomatoes, raise the heat a little and cook until most of the moisture has evaporated and the tomatoes have reduced to a thick pulp.

Beat the eggs together with the herbs and salt and pepper to taste and pour into the pan. Stir gently until they begin to set. Remove the pan from the heat while the mixture is still creamy. Serve garnished with the bread triangles.

Pipérade, aillade de Toulouse (page 112),
courgettes aux fines herbes (page 104)
and pissaladière (page 104).

Petits Pois A La Française *Peas Cooked with Lettuce*

NIVERNAIS

Tender young peas are a joy, and should be eaten, as they usually are in France, all alone, with their cooking juice, so that their full flavor is appreciated. This recipe can only be made in spring and early summer, when all the vegetables are young and fresh.

Preparation time: 10 minutes
Cooking time: 15 to 25 minutes
To serve: 4 to 6

$\frac{1}{4}$ *cup butter*
5 to 6 scallions, sliced
2 lettuce hearts, shredded
salt
freshly ground black pepper
3 lb fresh young peas, shelled
1 teaspoon sugar
$\frac{3}{4}$ *cup chicken broth or water*

Melt the butter in a heavy saucepan, add the scallions and allow them to soften. Add half the lettuce hearts and salt and pepper to taste, then stir in the peas. Sprinkle with the sugar and cover with the remaining shredded lettuce.

Pour in the broth or water and bring to a boil. Cover tightly and simmer for 10 to 20 minutes, or until the peas are just tender. Serve hot, with all the juice.

Haricots De Soissons A La Crème *Navy Beans in Cream Sauce*

ILE DE FRANCE

The beans from Soissons are the aristocrats of white beans. Small and pointed, with a slight green tinge, they are not only very pretty, but also have a special flavor. They are scarce and therefore expensive, but if you do find them, they will be fresh and should not need long soaking or cooking. They are much too good not to be eaten as a special side dish on their own.

Preparation time: 15 minutes plus soaking
*   time*
Cooking time: about 1 hour
To serve: 6

1 lb dried navy beans, soaked in cold water
*   for 4 to 5 hours*
1 bouquet garni
2 tablespoons butter
1 small onion, finely chopped
$\frac{1}{4}$ *lb Canadian bacon, finely diced*
$\frac{3}{4}$ *cup crème fraîche (see page 118) or heavy*
*   cream*
salt
freshly ground black pepper
1 tablespoon chopped fresh parsley

Drain the beans and put them into a saucepan with enough fresh cold water to cover. Add the bouquet garni, bring to a boil and simmer gently for at least 45 minutes until the beans are tender but have not lost their shape. Drain and keep warm.

Melt the butter in a heavy saucepan, add the onion and bacon and cook until the onion is soft. Add the beans and turn well to mix with the onion and bacon. Stir in the cream and bring just to a boil. Simmer until the cream has thickened a little.

Add salt and pepper to taste and sprinkle with parsley before serving.

Pissaladière *Onion, Anchovy and Olive Quiche*

PROVENCE

The pungent Provençal first cousin to the Italian Pizza, serve *pissaladière* as an appetizer, or as a light luncheon dish, accompanied by a salad.

Preparation time: 40 minutes plus 1 hour rising
Cooking time: 50 minutes
Oven temperature: 400°; reduced to 375°
To serve: 6

Dough
1 cake (0.6 oz) compressed yeast
2 tablespoons lukewarm water
1¼ cups flour
salt
1 egg, beaten
1 tablespoon olive oil

Filling
¼ cup olive oil
1¼ lb onions, thinly sliced
salt
freshly ground black pepper
1 can (2 oz) anchovy fillets, drained and
    halved
½ cup pitted ripe olives

Dissolve the yeast in the water and leave in a warm place until frothy. Sift the flour and salt into a warmed bowl, and make a well in the center. Add the yeast mixture, egg and olive oil and mix together with a wooden spoon. Knead the dough until it is springy and comes away from the sides of the bowl. Leave in a warm place to rise for about 1 hour, or until it has doubled in bulk. Meanwhile, heat the olive oil in a heavy skillet, add the onions and fry gently until they are quite soft and yellow. Do not allow them to brown. Season to taste with salt and pepper.

When the dough has risen, knead again, form into a ball and place on a well-oiled 12 inch round baking pan. Gently press the dough from the center outwards until the baking pan is evenly covered. Spread on the onions, then make a criss-cross pattern on top with the halved anchovy fillets and intersperse with the olives. Leave to rise again for 15 minutes, then place in the oven. Bake for 40 to 50 minutes, turning down the oven temperature for the last 15 minutes if the crust is turning too dark.

Cut into pieces before serving.

Courgettes Aux Fines Herbes *Zucchini with Herbs*

PROVENCE

This dish from Provence is made with fresh herbs, which bring out the delicate flavor of the zucchini.

Preparation time: 10 minutes (plus 1 hour draining)
Cooking time: 10 to 15 minutes
To serve: 4 to 6

2 lb zucchini, shredded
salt
3 tablespoons olive oil
large squeeze of lemon juice
1 tablespoon finely chopped fresh basil and
    parsley
freshly ground black pepper

Spread out the zucchini on a clean towel. Sprinkle with salt, then leave to drain in the towel in a colander for 1 hour. Squeeze out all the moisture through the towel.

Heat the oil in a skillet, add the zucchini and cook over a medium heat until they are tender, stirring from time to time. Sprinkle with lemon juice and herbs, season to taste with salt and pepper and toss gently before serving.

Ratatouille *Provençal Vegetable Ragoût*

PROVENCE

A specialty of Provence, ratatouille can be found, with local variations, all around the Mediterranean coast. It can be eaten hot or cold, on its own as an hors d'oeuvre or as a vegetable side dish, and goes equally well with fish or meat.

Preparation time: 30 minutes (plus 1 hour draining the vegetables)
Cooking time: 1 hour
To serve: 6 to 8

1 lb eggplants, sliced
1 lb zucchini, sliced
salt
¾ cup olive oil
3 large onions, sliced
2 garlic cloves, finely chopped
3 sweet peppers (mixed red and green, if possible), cored, seeded and cut into strips
1 lb tomatoes, peeled and seeded
salt
freshly ground black pepper
½ teaspoon sugar
2 tablespoons finely chopped fresh parsley or basil and parsley

Sprinkle the eggplants and the zucchini liberally with salt and leave in separate colanders to drain for 1 hour. When they are ready, rinse, squeeze out excess moisture and pat dry.

Heat the oil in a heavy saucepan, add the onions and garlic and fry until softened. Add the eggplants and cook, stirring well, until they become soft and yellow.

Add the zucchini and peppers, cover and cook gently for 30 minutes. Stir in the tomatoes, seasoning and sugar, and cook, uncovered, for a further 30 minutes. The vegetables should be soft and well mixed but retain their shapes, and most of the liquid should be evaporated. Stir in the parsley and basil before serving.

Haricots Verts A La Lyonnaise *Green Beans with Onions*

LYONNAISE

The designation "Lyonnaise" usually means that the recipe is prepared with onions, and this tangy preparation of green beans is no exception. The vinegar gives that extra fillip of flavor.

Preparation time: 10 minutes
Cooking time: 20 minutes
To serve: 4

1 lb small stringless green beans
salt
6 tablespoons butter
½ lb onions, thinly sliced
freshly ground black pepper
2 teaspoons vinegar
chopped fresh parsley

Wash the beans and place in a saucepan of boiling salted water. Bring to a boil, then simmer for 10 minutes. Drain the beans thoroughly and dry them with paper towels.

Melt the butter in a pan, add the onions and cook until golden. Add the beans and cook over a low heat until the beans have browned slightly. Add salt and pepper to taste, then the vinegar. Toss the ingredients together and transfer to a heated serving dish. Sprinkle with the parsley.

Salade De Lentilles *Lentil Salad*

LANGUEDOC

Made with the little green lentils of Puy, this is an excellent winter salad. Use the new season's lentils only, and they will not need very long to soak or cook.

Preparation time: 10 minutes (plus soaking)
Cooking time: 45 minutes to $1\frac{1}{4}$ hours
To serve: 6

1 to $1\frac{1}{2}$ cups lentils, soaked in cold water for a
  few hours and drained
1 large onion, peeled
2 cloves
1 carrot, peeled
1 bouquet garni
$\frac{3}{4}$ cup sauce vinaigrette (see page 110)
$\frac{1}{4}$ lb cervelat or salami, diced
1 large onion, or 1 bunch of scallions, finely
  chopped
1 garlic clove, finely chopped
1 tablespoon finely chopped fresh parsley

Put the lentils into a large saucepan with the onion stuck with the cloves, the carrot and bouquet garni. Cover with plenty of cold water, bring to a boil and simmer until just tender. Drain well, remove the onion, carrot and bouquet garni and tip the lentils into a salad bowl. Pour over the sauce vinaigrette and stir well. Leave to cool.

Stir in the sausage, chopped onion and garlic and sprinkle with the parsley before serving.

Les Lentilles De Puy Au Petit Salé *Lentils with Salt Pork*

LANGUEDOC

The little gray-green and slate colored lentils of Puy, in the northern part of the Languedoc, are well known for their flavor. They turn brown when cooked, but keep their shape well, and are excellent for simple winter dishes such as this one, which can be served on its own or as an appetizer or side dish.
The fresher the lentils are, the less soaking or cooking time they will need.

Preparation time: 10 minutes (plus soaking)
Cooking time: 45 minutes to $1\frac{1}{2}$ hours
To serve: 6

2 tablespoons butter
1 onion, finely chopped
1 garlic clove, finely chopped
$\frac{1}{2}$ lb piece of salt pork, soaked in cold water
  for a few hours, drained and diced
1 to $1\frac{1}{2}$ cups lentils, soaked in cold water for a
  few hours or overnight and drained
1 bouquet garni
salt
freshly ground black pepper
squeeze of lemon juice
1 tablespoon finely chopped fresh parsley

Melt the butter in a large heavy saucepan, add the onion and garlic and fry until softened. Add the diced pork and turn well. Stir in the lentils. Cover with plenty of cold water, add the bouquet garni and bring to a boil. Simmer until the lentils are tender.

Drain off the liquid and remove the bouquet garni. Adjust the seasoning, add the lemon juice, sprinkle with the parsley and serve hot.

Cèpes A La Bordelaise

Mushrooms Cooked in Oil with Shallots and Garlic

GUYENNE

The area around Bordeaux is particularly rich in mushrooms and especially the wonderfully-flavored cèpes. If these are not available, cultivated or field mushrooms will also be very good cooked in this way. Serve as a garnish or on croûtes of fried bread as a first course.

Preparation time: 10 minutes
Cooking time: 10 to 12 minutes
To serve: 2 to 3

2 tablespoons olive oil
1 lb cèpes or other mushrooms, sliced
salt
freshly ground black pepper
large squeeze of lemon juice
2 tablespoons finely chopped shallots
2 garlic cloves, finely chopped
2 tablespoons finely chopped fresh parsley

Heat the oil in a small skillet and add the cèpes. Cook over a moderate heat, stirring, until they soften. Raise the heat a little to evaporate any excess juice. Season to taste with salt and pepper and add the lemon juice.

Mix the shallots, garlic and parsley together and sprinkle over the cèpes in the pan. Do not stir, but allow to cook gently for 2 to 3 minutes. Serve hot.

Chou Rouge A La Limousine *Braised Red Cabbage with Chestnuts*

MARCHE AND LIMOUSINE

This classic red cabbage dish goes particularly well with the game and duck which are plentiful in the region. When poultry and meat dishes are served with a garnish of red cabbage, they are also described as *à la Limousine*.

Preparation time: 15 minutes
Cooking time: 3½ hours
Oven temperature: 325°
To serve: 10

¼ lb slab bacon, diced
1 medium-size onion, finely chopped
3 lb red cabbage, shredded
1½ cups red wine
1¼ cups beef broth
3 tablespoons wine vinegar
3 large bay leaves
5 cloves
⅛ teaspoon grated nutmeg
1 teaspoon salt
freshly ground black pepper
½ lb dried chestnuts or 1 large can of whole chestnuts in water, drained

If you are using dried chestnuts, soak in water overnight. Drain and use as directed below.

In a heavy flameproof casserole, cook the bacon over medium heat, stirring frequently, until all the fat has run out and the bacon is light brown. Remove the bacon with a slotted spoon and set aside. Cook the onions in the fat, stirring frequently, until soft and golden. Add the cabbage gradually, stirring after each addition to coat with the fat and onions. Cover the casserole tightly and cook over a low heat for 10 minutes.

Add the wine, broth, vinegar, bay leaves, cloves, nutmeg, salt, pepper and the reserved bacon to the cabbage. Cover again and cook in the oven for 2 hours, checking occasionally to make sure that there is sufficient liquid to keep the cabbage from burning. Add the chestnuts and cook for a further 1 hour. The juice should have reduced to a minimum; if it has not, remove the lid and cook a little longer until it does. Adjust the seasoning and serve. The dish is even better if it is cooked a day or two ahead of time and reheated when it is needed.

108

Sauces,
Pastry and
Fondues

Sauce Vinaigrette *French Salad Dressing*

The most classic and simple of all the salad dressings, this should be freshly made each time, using only the best ingredients. These will vary, however, from one area of France to another: in Normandy or Brittany a cider vinegar might be used instead of a wine one; in the south, pure olive oil is more likely to be used than a corn or nut oil or a combination of oils. The addition of garlic is optional, and becomes stronger the further south you go.

This sauce is frequently served separately, with salads or cold, cooked vegetables. A green lettuce salad, however, is usually dressed just before serving, and well tossed so that every leaf is thinly coated with the dressing.

Preparation time: about 3 minutes
Makes: about ½ cup

½ *garlic clove (optional)*
½ *teaspoon salt*
freshly ground black pepper
¼ *teaspoon sugar*
½ *teaspoon Dijon-style mustard (optional)*
2 tablespoons wine vinegar
6 tablespoons oil

Crush the garlic with the salt and mix in the pepper, sugar and mustard to make a smooth paste. Stir in the vinegar, then slowly add the oil, stirring all the time to amalgamate and make a smooth thick sauce.

Adjust the seasoning before serving.

Sauce Mousseline *Butter, Egg Yolk and Cream Sauce*

Even richer, yet lighter than a sauce hollandaise, this makes a real feast of a simple dish of asparagus.

Preparation time: 15 minutes
Cooking time: 15 to 20 minutes
To serve: 6

3 egg yolks
1 tablespoon lemon juice
1 tablespoon cold water
¾ *cup unsalted butter, cut into small cubes*
¾ *cup crème fraîche (see page 118)*
salt
white pepper

Make a hollandaise sauce (as on page 113). Just before serving, whip the crème fraîche lightly until it just begins to thicken, and fold into the finished hollandaise.

Season to taste with salt and pepper before serving.

Sauce mousseline and sauce vinaigrette

Beurre de Montpellier *Montpellier Butter*

LANGUEDOC

A lovely accompaniment to any poached or broiled fish. Montpellier butter is also good on chops or steaks, and for stuffed eggs.

Preparation time: 15 minutes
To serve: 6 to 8

¼ *lb bulk fresh spinach, or 2 oz frozen*
   spinach
bunch of watercress
small bunch of fresh parsley
2 sprigs of fresh tarragon
2 tablespoons capers
6 anchovy fillets
3 hard-cooked egg yolks
½ *cup butter*
1 tablespoon olive oil
large squeeze of lemon juice
freshly ground black pepper (optional)

Blanch the spinach, watercress and herbs together in boiling water for 1 minute. If you are using frozen spinach, you need only thaw it. Drain well, squeezing out as much moisture as possible, then put in a mortar or blender with the capers, anchovies and egg yolks. Pound or blend to a fine paste. If you are using a mortar, you may need to push the mixture through a nylon sieve.

Blend in the butter and then the oil, drop by drop, as for making mayonnaise. Add the lemon juice and test for seasoning. This is very unlikely to need salt, but may be improved by a little freshly ground black pepper.

111

Beurre Blanc *White Butter Sauce*

MAINE

This rich and velvety sauce of delicately flavored butter is also known as Beurre Nantais, and is traditionally served with pike or trout in the Loire country. It is equally popular in Brittany, where it is served just as frequently with steamed or broiled sea fish.

Preparation time: 15 minutes
Cooking time: 20 minutes
To serve: 6

5 tablespoons white wine
5 tablespoons wine vinegar
1 tablespoon finely chopped shallots
1½ cups (¾ lb) butter, at room temperature
salt
freshly ground black pepper
squeeze of lemon juice

Put the wine and vinegar in a small heavy saucepan with the shallots and boil until reduced to about 1 tablespoon. Remove from the heat.

Cut the butter into very small pieces (at least 20) and begin to add these one by one to the pan, beating with a wire whisk or rotary beater. Add each piece of butter only when the previous one has been completely absorbed and return the pan to a very gentle heat after the first few pieces of butter have been incorporated. Remove from the heat as soon as all the butter has been added, and stir in salt and pepper to taste and the lemon juice. Serve warm.

If the sauce is not to be served immediately, place it in a water bath or a double boiler to keep it at just the right temperature – if it becomes too cold, it will congeal; if too hot, it will separate.

Aillade De Toulouse *Walnut and Garlic Sauce*

LANGUEDOC

A rich, thick liaison of walnuts, garlic and oil, this is sometimes eaten just with some bread dipped in or with crisp vegetables as an hors d'oeuvre, but it is also served as a sauce with cold meat, poultry or ham.

Preparation time: 10 to 15 minutes
To serve: 6

¼ lb (about 1½ cups) walnuts
2 large garlic cloves
salt
freshly ground black pepper
about 5 tablespoons olive oil
squeeze of lemon juice (optional)

Pound, grind or blend the walnuts together with the garlic to form a smooth paste. Season to taste with salt and pepper.

Add the oil drop by drop, stirring or blending continuously as for making mayonnaise, until you have a smooth thick sauce. Adjust the seasoning and add a little lemon juice to taste, if liked.

Sauce Hollandaise *Butter and Egg Yolk Sauce*

This rich but light sauce is delicious with fish, or with such delicate vegetables as asparagus, artichokes or broccoli. It is also excellent served with eggs: the legendary *oeufs benedictine* is merely a poached egg lying on a buttered round of toast or cooked pastry, with a slice on ham on top, and coated with a sauce hollandaise. It is really not difficult to make, provided you give yourself fully to the task.

Preparation time: 10 minutes
Cooking time: 15 to 20 minutes
To serve: 6

3 egg yolks
1 tablespoon lemon juice
1 tablespoon cold water
¾ cup unsalted butter, cut into small cubes
salt
white pepper

Beat the egg yolks with the lemon juice and water in the top of a double boiler until they become quite thick and pale. An electric beater is invaluable for this. Place over the bottom pan of simmering water and beat in the little cubes of butter, one at a time. Do not add the next piece of butter until the previous one has been fully absorbed. Season to taste with salt and pepper before serving.

You can keep the sauce warm for up to 1 hour by setting the top pan in a water bath that is kept just above lukewarm – if it is allowed to become too hot, the sauce will curdle; if too cold, it will begin to harden.

There is a short-cut way of making this sauce which is almost as good: put the egg yolks, lemon juice and water into a blender and process until smooth. Heat the butter in a saucepan until it just begins to froth, then, keeping the blender at full speed, slowly drip in the butter until it has all been absorbed and the sauce has thickened. Season to taste with salt and pepper before serving.

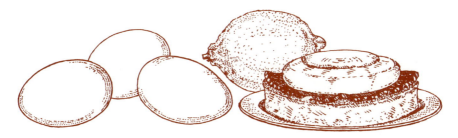

Sauce Béarnaise *Herbed Butter Sauce*

BEARN

This sauce is not really a native of Béarn, but it is said to have been invented for Henri IV and named after his native land. It is excellent with chicken, steak or fish.

Preparation time: 20 minutes
Cooking time: 15 to 20 minutes
To serve: 6

5 tablespoons wine vinegar
5 tablespoons water
2 fresh tarragon branches
2 shallots, finely chopped
1 strip of lemon rind
6 peppercorns, lightly crushed
3 egg yolks
¾ cup unsalted butter, diced

Put the vinegar and water into a small saucepan, add the tarragon, shallots, lemon rind and peppercorns and boil fiercely until the liquid is reduced to about 2 tablespoons. Strain.

Put the egg yolks into the top of a double boiler and beat until thick and fluffy. Beat in the liquid. Place over the bottom pan of simmering water and slowly add the butter, piece by piece, beating each one in until absorbed before adding the next. Season to taste with salt and pepper before serving.

You can also use a short-cut method of making this sauce, using the method given for sauce hollandaise above.

Pâte Brisée *Pie Pastry*

This is the standard French pastry for quiches and tarts. It is light and crisp, and should be handled as little and as lightly as possible. The proportion of fat to flour is very high, and the pastry is consequently rather fragile. You can, of course, vary this proportion a little, but the pastry will not be quite as delicate.

The following quantities make sufficient dough to line two 10 to 12 inch flan or quiche pans. The dough keeps in the refrigerator for at least a week, or for about 3 months in the freezer.

Preparation time: 10 minutes (plus 1 hour resting)

$1\frac{1}{4}$ *cups flour*
pinch of salt
pinch of confectioners' sugar
$\frac{1}{2}$ *cup butter, preferably unsalted*
a little iced water

Sift the flour onto a pastry board together with the salt and sugar. Cut the butter into small pieces and cut into the flour, then rub in with the fingertips until the mixture resembles fine bread crumbs. Sprinkle with a little iced water, then gather together into a ball with one hand.

Sprinkle a little flour onto the board and, using the heel of your hand, quickly spread the dough away from you onto the floured board. This will ensure that the butter is evenly distributed. This whole operation should be done as quickly and lightly as possible. Gather up into a ball again and leave in the refrigerator to rest for at least 1 hour.

Leave the dough at room temperature for a little while before rolling out, so that it becomes malleable again. If it is very hard at first, hit it with a rolling pin, but do not knead again.

Pâte Brisée Sucrée

Sweetened Pie Pastry

Make this in the same way as the pâte brisée, but instead of adding only a pinch of confectioners' sugar, add $\frac{1}{4}$ cup granulated or $\frac{1}{2}$ cup confectioners' sugar.

Gougère

BURGUNDY

Served with a good bottle of red Burgundy, this simple dish makes an excellent first course, or a light lunch or supper dish. To make it more substantial, you can fill the center with a delicate green vegetable, covered with a sauce hollandaise (see page 113).

Preparation time: 20 minutes
Cooking time: 35 to 40 minutes
Oven temperature: 375°
To serve: 4 to 6

$1\frac{1}{4}$ *cups milk*
$\frac{1}{2}$ *cup butter*
salt
white pepper
1 cup flour, sifted
4 eggs
$\frac{1}{4}$ *lb Gruyère or Comté cheese, diced*

Gougère

Pâte Feuilletée Puff Pastry

Put the milk into a heavy saucepan together with the butter cut into small pieces and salt and pepper to taste. Heat slowly, stirring, until the butter has melted, then bring rapidly to a boil to combine. As soon as the milk is boiling, take the pan off the heat and tip in all the flour. Stir rapidly with a wooden spoon to form a smooth paste. Return to a moderate heat and stir until the mixture forms a ball and leaves the sides of the pan clean.

Take off the heat and beat in the eggs one by one. When the last egg has been absorbed and the mixture is smooth and glossy, stir in all but 1 tablespoon of the diced cheese.

Butter a tube or savarin pan and spoon in the mixture evenly. Scatter the remaining cheese over the top.

Bake until the top has risen, is golden brown and just firm to the touch. Turn out of the pan carefully and serve immediately, very hot.

Although frozen puff pastry or patty shells can be used for all the recipes requiring pâte feuilletée, it takes only a little while to learn to make this "pastry of a thousand leaves" yourself, and the effort is very worthwhile, as the results are infinitely more melting on the tongue. If at first you don't achieve the desired standard of perfection, do try again – it is a knack you will learn.

The dough keeps in the refrigerator for at least a week, or 3–4 months in the freezer.

Preparation time: 30 minutes (plus 4 to 5
  hours resting)
Makes: about 1½ lb

4 cups flour
½ teaspoon salt
2 tablespoons corn or nut oil
about ¾ cup iced water
¾ cup butter, preferably unsalted

Sift the flour and salt into a mixing bowl, sprinkle on the oil and most of the water, and begin to mix with a wooden spoon or spatula. Start to gather up the dough with one hand, sprinkling on a little more water as necessary to make a workable dough, but not one that is damp or sticky. When you have a ball of dough, sprinkle it with a little flour and leave to rest in the refrigerator for 30 minutes.

Remove from the refrigerator and roll or pat out into a rectangle three times as long as it is wide on a lightly floured surface.

Place the butter between two sheets of wax paper and beat it into a flat rectangle, using a rolling pin. Place the butter on a lightly floured surface, sprinkle with more flour and work it into smooth, pliable consistency, using the ball of the hand. Spread the butter onto the two thirds of the dough furthest away from you, leaving a narrow margin all around.

Fold the third that is nearest to you over towards the center and then fold over again. Give the package a quarter turn. Sprinkle the working surface and the dough with a little flour and roll out firmly away from yourself to form another long rectangle. Fold both ends of the rectangle towards the center, then fold over to make a neat package. Refrigerate the dough for about 1 hour.

Repeat the process of twice rolling and folding the dough once more.

Let the dough rest a few minutes at room temperature when you take it out of the refrigerator, and if it still seems too firm to roll out at first, beat it lightly with the rolling pin before rolling out. After the fourth turn refrigerate the dough again for at least 1 hour before using.

Fondue Aux Trois Fromages *Cheese Fondue*

FRANCHE-COMTE

You need a cheese fondue set, or at least an alcohol table burner that will hold your casserole on the table, to serve this dish, which is not just a meal but also an entertainment. Cheese fondues are eaten in Switzerland, as well as in the Franche-Comté and in the Savoie – the only slight difference is in the local cheeses used. If the selection of cheeses given below is unobtainable, use whatever hard, melting cheeses are available. When the fondue is ready it is set in the center of the table, over a flame. Everyone has a long-handled fork on which to spear the cubes of bread and dip them into the fondue.

Preparation time: 15 minutes
Cooking time: 20 minutes
To serve: 6

1 garlic clove, halved
$\frac{1}{2}$ lb Comté cheese, thinly sliced
$\frac{1}{2}$ lb Gruyère cheese, thinly sliced
$\frac{1}{2}$ lb Beaufort cheese, thinly sliced
$1\frac{1}{4}$ cups white wine
freshly ground black pepper
1 teaspoon cornstarch
3 tablespoons kirsch
8 to 12 slices of day old white bread, cubed,
   for serving

Rub the clove of garlic firmly around the inside of a flameproof casserole. Put the cheeses and the wine into the casserole and stir over a moderate heat until all the cheese has melted. Season liberally with pepper.

Stir the cornstarch and kirsch together to make a smooth paste. Add to the casserole and stir until you have a smooth, well combined cream. Bring to a boil, then transfer, still gently bubbling, to the burner on the table.

The fondue will continue to cook gently as you eat, and the mixture will get thicker as you get lower in the dish. Add a little more kirsch at the end if you like.

The thin crust which will have formed on the bottom of the casserole is a special *bonne bouche* and should be shared equally between the participants.

Fondue De Fromage A Brillat-Savarin *Cheese and Egg Fondue*

SAVOIE

Brillat-Savarin is one of the most famous names in French gastronomy. He was a native of the Savoie, and his recipes and preferences often reflect the influence of that heritage. His classic work *The Psychology of Taste* (1826) was more a celebration of good living and good food than a conventional cookbook. This recipe is an approximation of a dish he describes, and would serve for a late supper or snack.

Preparation time: 10 minutes
Cooking time: 15 minutes
To serve: 6

12 eggs
$\frac{1}{2}$ cup+2 tablespoons butter
$2\frac{1}{2}$ cups grated Gruyère cheese
salt
freshly ground black pepper
toast (optional)

Break the eggs into a heavy saucepan and beat thoroughly. Melt the butter, cool slightly and add to the eggs. Stir in the grated cheese. Place the saucepan over a high heat and begin stirring the fondue vigorously with a wooden spoon. After a few minutes, turn the heat down slightly, but continue stirring. When the mixture begins thickening, watch it carefully so that it does not stick. Add a pinch of salt and plenty of pepper just before the fondue reaches the desired consistency. It will appear like slightly more granular scrambled eggs. Serve on toast or – alternatively and more classically – by itself on heated plates. Accompany with French bread, pickled onions and a green salad.

116

Sorbets,
Fruit Desserts
and Sweets

Coeur A La Crème *Cream Cheese Dessert*

NORMANDY

Light, delicate and refreshing, this may be eaten with cream, or with soft summer fruit. This dessert takes its name from the small heart-shaped white porcelain colanders in which it was originally made.

Preparation time: 20 minutes (plus draining overnight)
To serve: 4 to 6

½ lb (about 1 cup) cottage cheese
1¼ cups crème fraîche (see page 118)
2 tablespoons caster sugar
2 egg whites
1¼ cups light cream for serving

Pass the cheese through a nylon sieve. Lightly whip the cream with the sugar and mix into the cheese. Beat the egg whites until stiff and fold into the cheese mixture. Turn into the muslin, cheesecloth or paper towel lined mold, colander or sieve. Leave to drain overnight in the refrigerator.

Unmold, pour over the cream and serve.

Crème Fraîche *Lightly Soured Cream*

NORMANDY

In France cream is generally left to mature so that the lactic acids remain active and give it a very slightly sour taste. It is known as crème fraîche and is particularly good for cooking, as it lends a slight tang to savory dishes, and acts as a very good thickener. It keeps better than fresh cream – 10 to 14 days in the refrigerator – though it will become thicker as time goes on.

Preparation time: 5 to 10 minutes (plus thickening)
Makes: about 2½ cups

2 tablespoons sour cream or buttermilk
2½ cups heavy cream

Stir the sour cream or buttermilk into the cream and heat very gently until lukewarm. The cream should still feel slightly cool to the back of the finger – the correct maximum temperature is 85°. Pour into an earthenware bowl, cover and leave in a warm place to thicken. This will take from 5 to 24 hours, depending on the temperature. Refrigerate. *Note:* If crème fraîche is not available when called for in recipes, it can be replaced by heavy cream, lightly soured with a little lemon juice, or by a mixture of heavy cream and sour cream.

Sorbet De Champagne *Champagne Sherbet*

CHAMPAGNE

This is a light and refreshing way to end a very special meal on a festive occasion.

Preparation time: 10 minutes (plus 3 hours minimum freezing)
Cooking time: 5 minutes
To serve: 6

2½ cups water
1 cup sugar
1 vanilla bean
finely pared rind and juice of 1 lemon
2½ cups Champagne
12 langues de chats for serving

Put the water, sugar, vanilla bean and lemon rind in a saucepan and bring to a boil, stirring to dissolve the sugar. Boil for 5 minutes. Strain and leave to cool.

Add the lemon juice and pour into an ice-tray. Put into the freezer. Freeze until set but still soft and mushy.

Turn into a chilled bowl and mash lightly with a fork until smooth. Mix in the Champagne. Return quickly to the freezer and leave until frozen.

Serve straight from the freezer in chilled Champagne glasses, accompanied by langues de chats.

Coeur à la crème and crème fraîche

Mousse Au Chocolat *Chocolate Mousse*

ILE DE FRANCE

Chocolat Menier, one of the best of cooking chocolates, has been made in a factory at Noisiel on the Marne, not far from Paris, since the house was founded in 1825. Use Menier chocolate if you can for this extremely simple and unfailingly popular recipe, and make the mousse a day ahead to give it time to settle, and for the flavor to mature.

Preparation time: 30 minutes (plus chilling)
To serve: 6

7 oz semisweet or bitter chocolate, broken
　　into pieces
6 eggs, separated
2 tablespoons brandy
¾ cup whipped cream to decorate (optional)

Put the chocolate into the top of a double boiler, set this over simmering water and leave until the chocolate has melted. Remove from the heat and beat in the egg yolks one by one with a wooden spoon. The mixture will be very stiff at first, but it will become soft and smooth as you continue to add the yolks. Stir in the brandy.

Beat the egg whites until they are stiff but not dry. Stir one-third into the chocolate mixture until completely combined, then lightly fold the chocolate mixture into the remaining egg whites, using a spatula or metal spoon. Pour into a serving dish and refrigerate overnight.

You can decorate the mousse with swirls of whipped cream before serving if you wish.

Cotignac Orléannais *Quince Paste*

ORLEANNAIS

This beautiful, opaque, deep amber pink quince paste is a specialty of the town of Orléans. It may be kept in sterilized jars, like a preserve, or in the freezer. It can be eaten alone, or with a little crème chantilly (see page 121), and it is especially good served with cream cheese or coeur à la crème (see page 118).

Preparation time: about 1 hour
Cooking time: about 2½ hours

7 lb quinces
2 large oranges
about 4 cups sugar

Quarter and core half the quinces and cut them into small chunks. Put them in a large saucepan. Add enough water to cover, bring to a boil and simmer for about 1 hour, or until soft. Strain through a jelly bag squeezing out as much juice as possible.

Peel, core and slice the remaining quinces. Put them into a clean saucepan with the quince juice. Cut the oranges in half, scoop out the flesh and squeeze out any remaining juice. Add the flesh and juice to the quinces, with enough water to come just to the top of the fruit mixture. Bring to a boil and simmer until very soft and almost puréed.

Process the quince purée in a blender and then pass through a nylon sieve, so that no gritty parts remain. Measure the purée and return to the clean saucepan with an equal quantity of sugar. Cook over a moderate heat, stirring frequently to prevent it from sticking to the bottom of the pan, until the purée is very thick and beginning to come away from the sides of the saucepan. Cool and store in sterilized canning jars or freezer containers.

Crème Chantilly *Whipped Cream*

ILE DE FRANCE

The little town of Chantilly, some few miles north of Paris, famous for its rich pastures, has become associated forever with the lightly whipped, slightly soured cream that tops the best pâtisseries and desserts throughout France. Made with crème fraîche it has a pleasing slight acidity. Because crème fraîche can become very stiff, iced water needs to be added before it can be whipped, and it becomes therefore very light and airy, and much more delicate than our whipped cream.

Preparation time: 10 to 15 minutes

1¼ cups crème fraîche (see page 118)
2 to 4 tablespoons iced water
about 2 teaspoons vanilla sugar or
  confectioners' sugar
1 egg white, stiffly beaten (optional)

Whip the crème fraîche with a balloon whisk, adding the water gradually according to how stiff the cream is. Whip in sugar to taste towards the end, but remember that the cream should not be really sweet. If you want to use the cream in large quantities, you can fold in the stiffly beaten egg white at the end.

Crème chantilly may be put on the table in bowls so that everyone can serve themselves, or piped onto desserts in decorative patterns.

Petits Pots Au Chocolat *Chocolate Creams*

ILE DE FRANCE

These individual creams take their name from the little pot-bellied, two-handled pots, brown on the outside and white inside, in which they are traditionally served. The cream is very quick and simple to make, and is a perfect ending for a special meal. Although light, it is quite rich, and this quantity serves 4 generously.

Preparation time: 10 minutes (plus setting)
Cooking time: 3 minutes
To serve: 4

1¼ cups light cream
7 oz semisweet or bitter chocolate, broken
  into pieces
pinch of salt
1 teaspoon vanilla
1 egg, beaten

Scald the cream. Remove from the heat and add the chocolate. Stir until the chocolate has completely melted and the mixture is quite smooth. Add the salt and vanilla and stir in the egg.

Alternatively, if you have a blender, pour the scalded cream onto the chocolate in the blender goblet and blend until smooth. Blend in the remaining ingredients.

Pour into the individual pots and leave to set for at least 4 hours in the refrigerator.

Poires Au Cassis *Pears in Cassis*

BURGUNDY

An unusual and refreshing way of preparing pears, this uses the local black currant liqueur.

Preparation time: 15 minutes (plus chilling)
Cooking time: 15 to 30 minutes
To serve: 6

6 large pears
1 cup sugar
2 cups water
1 vanilla bean
¾ cup crème de cassis
juice of ½ to 1 lemon

Peel the pears, leaving them whole and as far as possible with the stalks on.

Bring the sugar and water to a boil in a wide saucepan, stirring until the sugar has dissolved. Add the vanilla bean. Lower the pears gently into the syrup. They should all be covered by the liquid, so add a little more water if necessary. Simmer gently until the pears are tender, but take care not to overcook, as they must not be allowed to disintegrate.

When done, lift the pears out gently with a slotted spoon and place in a serving dish. Pour over the cassis.

Bring the syrup left in the pan to a boil and boil fiercely to reduce to about half the original quantity. Add lemon juice to taste and pour over the pears. Chill before serving.

Oeufs A La Neige

Poached Meringues with Custard

BURGUNDY

This delicate dessert is much loved by children. To make it more sophisticated you can sprinkle it with finely crushed praline.

Preparation time: 40 minutes (plus chilling)
Cooking time: 30 minutes
To serve: 4 to 6

4 eggs, separated
½ cup+2 tablespoons sugar
2½ cups milk
2 tablespoons water
1 vanilla bean

Beat the egg whites until they stand in peaks. Slowly beat in 6 tablespoons of the sugar and continue to beat until very stiff.

Put the milk, water and vanilla bean in a wide saucepan and heat to just below boiling point. Using a large tablespoon, shape the meringue mixture into large egg shapes. Float these on top of the milk, a few at a time. After 2 minutes, turn them over and poach on the other side. Lift out with a slotted spoon and leave to drain in a wide dish.

When all the meringue mixture has been used, remove the vanilla bean from the milk. Beat the egg yolks with the remaining sugar, then slowly beat in a little of the milk. Stir this mixture into the milk in the saucepan and stir over a very low heat until the custard thickens. Pour the custard into a shallow serving dish, and top with the meringue "snowballs." Chill before serving.

Sorbet De Raisins *Grape Sherbet*

BURGUNDY

Made with ripe, sweet grapes, this is the perfect dessert to end a rich meal. It is light, refreshing, but by no means innocent!

Preparation time: 10 minutes (plus freezing)
Cooking time: 5 minutes
To serve: 4 to 6

1½ lb purple grapes
½ cup sugar (or a little more if the grapes
  are not very sweet)
1¼ cups water
squeeze of lemon juice
2 tablespoons brandy

Pluck the grapes off the stalks but do not bother to peel or seed. Put them into a blender and blend very briefly, then press through a nylon sieve to obtain all the juice and a little of the bitter flavor of the skins.

Put the sugar and water in a saucepan and bring to a boil, stirring to dissolve the sugar. Boil for 5 minutes. Cool, then stir into the grape juice. Add a little lemon juice and taste for sweetness – the mixture should taste a little over-sweet at this point. Pour into freezing trays and freeze.

When the mixture begins to set, mash it lightly with a fork or in a blender and blend in the brandy. Return to the freezer and freeze until hard, a minimum of 2 hours.

Serve in chilled wine glasses, straight from the freezer.

Poires au cassis, poirat de Berry (page 141),
soufflé glacé au kirsch (page 125) and oeufs à la neige

Gelée De Groseilles *Red Currant Jelly*

LORRAINE

The sunripened red currants of Lorraine make wonderful jams and jellies, and these are used as much for cooking as to spread on "tartines." Fruit tarts, in particular, are often glazed with a jelly made of the same fruit, or of one with contrasting flavor or color.

Preparation time: 30 minutes (plus straining overnight)
Cooking time: 5 to 10 minutes

red currants
sugar

Wash the red currants. Put into a large saucepan with just enough water to stop them burning. Bring slowly to a boil. Stir and lightly mash the fruit as it heats.

Remove the fruit from the heat and pour into a scalded jelly bag. Allow to drip overnight. Measure the juice and allow 4 cups of sugar to each quart of juice. Put into the pan and bring very slowly to a boil, stirring all the time so that the sugar dissolves evenly. Do not let it boil until the sugar has dissolved.

Boil for 5 minutes without stirring, then test by dropping a little of the jelly onto a cold saucer. When a skin forms as it cools, the jelly is ready.

Leave to cool a little in the pan, then remove any scum and pour into sterilized small jars. Seal and keep in a cool place.

Gelée De Groseilles A Froid *Uncooked Red Currant Jelly*

LORRAINE

These translucent jellies are potted in very small quantities in miniature glass jars, and kept as a great delicacy. They do not keep as well as the cooked jelly, but their flavor is quite miraculous, and small quantities, melted down to make a glaze or used in small blobs as decoration, transform a dessert. This recipe is only suitable for use when red currants are very plentiful and ripe.

Preparation time: 1 hour (plus straining overnight)

red currants, washed and stripped off the stalks
sugar

Put the red currants into a large bowl and crush them very gently with a wooden mallet or spoon. Put the contents of the bowl into a scalded jelly bag and allow to drip overnight. Measure the juice and measure out an equal quantity of sugar. Add the sugar little by little to the currant juice, stirring all the time so that the sugar dissolves. When all the sugar has dissolved, pour into small sterilized jars, cover and keep in a light, dry place.

Les Groseilles Au Jus De Framboise *Red Currants in Raspberry Juice*

ALSACE

This is a lovely tart, refreshing dessert. Its jewel colors look wonderful served in sparkling glasses on a sunny day.

Preparation time: 15 minutes (plus chilling)
Cooking time: 5 minutes
To serve: 4 to 6

2 pints red currants (or red and white currants mixed), stripped off the stalks
1 pint raspberries
$\frac{2}{3}$ cup sugar
squeeze of lemon juice

Pile the currants into individual long-stemmed wine glasses.

Put the raspberries and sugar into a heavy saucepan, crush them lightly and heat gently, so that the juice begins to run. Do not boil, as this alters the flavor of the fruit.

Pass the raspberry juice through a nylon sieve. Add the lemon juice and a little more sugar if necessary, depending on how tart the currants are. Pour the raspberry sauce over the currants in the glasses, chill and serve.

Sorbet De Framboises Et De Groseilles Raspberry and Red Currant Ice

ALSACE

French sorbets tend to be very light but slightly creamy – somewhere halfway between the Italian water ices and our ice creams. This is a particularly delicate and refreshing combination of fruit flavors.

Preparation time: 20 minutes (plus 2 hours minimum freezing)
Cooking time: 5 minutes
To serve: 6

3 cups raspberries
1 cup red currants
⅔ cup sugar
¾ cup water
¾ cup crème fraîche (see page 118) or heavy cream

Purée the raspberries and red currants together in a blender, then pass through a nylon sieve.

Dissolve the sugar in the water in a saucepan, then bring to a boil. Boil vigorously for 5 minutes, to make a syrup. Cool.

Stir the cooled syrup into the fruit purée followed by the cream and pour into a freezing tray. Put into the freezer.

When the mixture begins to set, remove it from the freezer and beat well, preferably with an electric beater or in a blender. Return to the freezer and leave to set.

Remove from the freezer and keep in the refrigerator for 1 hour before serving.

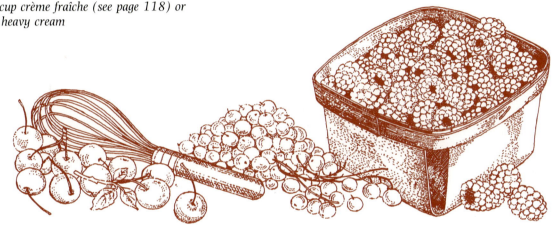

Soufflé Glacé Au Kirsch Iced Kirsch Soufflé

FRANCHE-COMTE

Kirschwasser, the brandy made from cherries, is the product of the Black Forest and the Vosges, the forested mountain regions that border France, and is used quite extensively in cooking in this part of France also. The following is a wonderfully rich but light dessert.

Preparation time: 20 minutes (plus freezing)
Cooking time: 3 to 5 minutes
To serve: 6

1 cup sugar
¾ cup water
4 egg whites
2 tablespoons Kirschwasser
1¼ cups crème fraîche (see page 118) or heavy cream

Dissolve the sugar in the water in a saucepan, then bring to a boil. Boil for 3 to 5 minutes or until a thick syrup is formed. Beat the egg whites until they stand in peaks, and, continuing to beat, pour in the syrup in a thin stream. Dribble in the Kirschwasser.

Whip the cream lightly until it is thick and bulky but not stiff. Fold into the soufflé mixture. Pour into a freezerproof glass serving dish and freeze until set.

Serve frozen.

Glace Au Miel *Honey Ice Cream*

PROVENCE

The herb-scented honeys of Provence give this ice cream a marvelous flavor. Unless you have one of these special honeys, it is worth using some fresh herbs to achieve the same tangy sweetness.

Preparation time: 20 minutes (plus 4 hours minimum freezing)
Cooking time: 10 minutes
To serve: 6

6 egg yolks
½ cup honey
1 fresh rosemary or thyme branch
1¼ cups milk or light cream
¾ cup crème fraîche (see page 118) or heavy cream

Beat the egg yolks until they are light and fluffy.

Heat the honey together with the rosemary or thyme until it just reaches boiling point. Remove the herb and pour the honey onto the yolks, beating well.

Scald the milk or cream and beat this into the honey mixture. Pour into a heavy saucepan and stir over a very gentle heat until the mixture begins to thicken. On no account allow it to boil. Remove from the heat and leave to cool.

Whip the cream until thick and bulky and fold into the cooled honey custard. Turn into a freezing tray or freezer-proof serving dish and freeze.

Remove from the freezer 15 minutes before serving.

Compôte De Fruits D'Hiver *Winter Fruit Salad*

PROVENCE

While Provence is a summer paradise, the winters can be cold and biting. A salad like this one, with its memory of the fruits of summer, can be very cheering.

Preparation time: 20 minutes (plus soaking)
Cooking time: 30 to 40 minutes
To serve: 6

1 cup prunes, soaked overnight, drained and pitted
⅔ cup dried apricots, soaked overnight and drained
⅔ cup dried peaches, soaked overnight and drained
4 small cooking pears, peeled
1¼ cups red wine
1 cinnamon stick
2 cloves
1 vanilla bean
about ¼ cup sugar
1 orange, peeled and sliced
6 walnuts, shelled and halved

Put all the prepared fruits except the orange into a heavy wide-bottomed saucepan and add the wine, spices, sugar and enough water just to cover the fruit. Poach until the fruit is tender.

Lift the fruit out with a slotted spoon and place in a serving dish. Add the orange slices and the walnut halves.

Bring the poaching liquid to a boil and boil rapidly until reduced by about half. Add more sugar to taste, strain over the fruit and leave to cool before serving.

Glace au miel, croquante and compôte de fruits d'hiver

Croquante *Almond Brittle*

PROVENCE

One of the traditional Christmas desserts of Provence, this is made in large sheets and sometimes shaped over a bowl to make a *cloche* or bell shape. This is then placed on the table and everyone can break off a piece as they wish.

If the mixture is simply left to cool and harden, it can be crushed to form a praline powder, to be used to flavor desserts and ices, or to decorate cakes.

Preparation time: 20 minutes
Cooking time: 10 minutes
Oven temperature: 350°
To serve: 6

1 lb almonds, blanched and roughly chopped (about 4 cups)
1 to 1⅓ cups sugar, brown or white, or a mixture of the two
6 tablespoons water

Toast the almonds gently in the oven or brown lightly under the broiler, until just pale golden brown.

Put the sugar into a heavy saucepan with the water and bring very gently to a boil, stirring until all the sugar has dissolved. Boil until the syrup reaches a temperature of 300° or until it turns golden brown. If you are using brown sugar, it is best to use a candy thermometer, as the color is deceptive.

Remove from the heat and add the almonds. Stir well so that they become evenly coated with the caramel. Pour quickly onto an oiled wooden board, and use the back of a wooden spoon to spread out as thinly as possible. You need to work fast as the mixture hardens quickly.

To make a bell shape, lift the sheet of brittle off as soon as it has set and mold over the back of a bowl. Remove the bowl and leave to cool.

If praline is needed, crush into a powder when the mixture is quite cold and hard.

Nougat *Honey and Almond Candy*

DAUPHINE

This is a specialty of the town of Montélimar, which borders on Provence, and indeed this confection relies on some of the products of Provence, with its herb and flower-scented honeys and pink-blossomed almond trees. In Montélimar you will see boxes of nougat in the confectioners' windows all the year through, but further south, in Nice, where they have their own version of nougat, it is a traditional part of the Christmas celebrations.

It is not difficult to master the art of making nougat, although a candy thermometer is probably essential. Once mastered, it is a most enjoyable pre-Christmas occupation.

Preparation time: 15 minutes (plus setting)
Cooking time: about 40 minutes
Oven temperature: 375° (optional)

1½ cups roughly chopped blanched almonds
2 egg whites
⅓ cup honey
½ cup sugar
2 tablespoons water
rice paper

Toast the almonds lightly under a broiler or in the oven.

Whisk the egg whites until they form soft peaks.

Heat the honey in a small heavy saucepan to 300°. In another saucepan, heat the sugar and water, stirring until the sugar has dissolved, then bring to a boil and boil until the syrup also reaches 300°. Mix the honey and syrup together. Carefully stir in the egg whites. Add the nuts, then slowly bring to a boil. Boil for 1 minute.

Line a loaf pan with foil and then with a sheet of rice paper. Pour in the nougat mixture, cover with another sheet of rice paper and weigh down. Leave at room temperature to cool and set for at least 12 hours before cutting into small squares or bars. Eat while fresh.

Parfait Marie *Iced Anisette Mousse*

GUYENNE

Anisette is the local liqueur made from aniseed, and it has a highly sophisticated flavor.

Preparation time: 20 minutes (plus freezing)
Cooking time: 5 minutes
To serve: 6

½ cup sugar
1¼ cups water
4 large egg yolks
¼ cup anisette
2 cups whipping cream

Dissolve the sugar in the water in a saucepan and bring to a boil. Boil briskly for 5 minutes.

Meanwhile beat the egg yolks with an electric beater until they are fluffy. Pour in the very hot sugar syrup in a thin stream and continue to beat at full speed until the mixture is cool. Beat in the anisette.

Whip the cream lightly, then fold into the egg mixture. Pour into a freezerproof serving dish or individual ramekin dishes and freeze for at least 4 hours.

Serve straight from the freezer.

Cakes, Crêpes and Pâtisseries

Les Crêpes Dentellées *Lacy Crêpes*

BRITTANY

If Brittany has a national dish, it must be crêpes, the huge buckwheat pancakes which can be bought at every street corner, to be eaten wrapped around a piece of local sausage, a lump of cheese, or with butter and sugar or jam. Crêperies are to be found in every little Breton town, and in these small restaurants you can make a whole meal of crêpes, washed down with the local cider, starting with savory fillings, such as seafood, ham or chicken, and working your way through cheese and fruit to a final crêpe au chocolat.

These buckwheat pancakes, though good if you are very hungry, can be rather heavy, and more attractive are the lacy little crêpes dentellées, the specialty of the town of Quimper.

Preparation time: 10 minutes
Cooking time: 20 minutes
To serve: 4 to 6

1 cup flour
½ cup confectioners' sugar
pinch of salt
1 large egg, lightly beaten
2 tablespoons butter, melted and cooled
1 tablespoon vegetable oil
1 tablespoon brandy
about ¾ cup warm water
oil for frying
sugar and orange or lemon juice for serving

Gâteau Breton *Breton Cake*

BRITTANY

This lovely plain but buttery cake is sold at street corners and in markets all over Brittany, and you can buy a slice to eat at any time of day. Have it with a cup of tea or coffee – or do as the Bretons do, and drink a glass of dry hard country cider with it.

Preparation time: 20 minutes
Cooking time: 1 hour 20 minutes
Oven temperature: 375°
To serve: 6 to 8

3 cups flour
¾ cup sugar
6 egg yolks
⅞ cup butter, at room temperature

Sift the flour, sugar and salt into a bowl, make a well in the center and add the egg, butter, oil and brandy. Gradually work the flour into the liquids, adding enough of the water to make a smooth, fairly thin batter.

Cook in a lightly oiled hot pan, to make small and very thin crêpes. As soon as the batter touches the pan, it will begin to form bubbles, which then become holes, making the crêpes look like lacy doilies.

Sprinkle with sugar and a little orange or lemon juice to serve.

Tarte Normande, pain perdu Normand and bourdelats Normande (page 132)

Sift the flour and sugar into a bowl and make a well in the center. Beat 5 of the egg yolks together lightly with a fork. Pour into the well and slowly work in the flour, using a wooden spoon at first, and then your fingertips to crumble together finely.

Cut the butter into small pieces and, using a palette knife at first and then your fingertips, work them into the mixture until you have a fine, crumbly pastry. Press into a well-buttered 9 inch flan or quiche pan. Brush over the top with the remaining egg yolk and trace a pattern with a fork.

Bake in the oven until the top is golden brown. Turn out and allow to cool before serving.

Pain Perdu Normand

French Toast and Apple Dessert
NORMANDY

This delicious dessert is made very quickly with simple ingredients.

Preparation time: 10 minutes
Cooking time: 8 minutes
To serve: 4

6 to 8 slices of stale white bread or brioche
3 tablespoons cider
1 egg, beaten
¼ cup butter
2 apples, peeled, cored and thinly sliced
2 tablespoons sugar
2 tablespoons Calvados

Spread out the slices of bread or brioche and sprinkle the cider over them. Leave to soak for a few minutes, then dip quickly into the egg so that both sides are lightly coated.

Melt the butter in a skillet. When foaming, add the slices of bread and fry quickly on one side. Turn over and add the apples. When the bread is golden brown on both sides, sprinkle with the sugar, pour on the warmed Calvados and set alight. Bring flaming to the table.

Les crêpes dentellées and gâteau Breton

Tarte Normande *Normandy Apple Tart*

NORMANDY

Of the dozens of ways of making apple tart known to the French housewife, this one uses the most apples – appropriately from a region famous for its apple orchards.

Preparation time: 30 minutes (plus pastry)
Cooking time: 35 minutes
Oven temperature: 425°
To serve: 6

1 quantity pâte brisée sucrée (see page 114)
2 lb tart apples
about ¾ cup water
2 tablespoons butter
¼ cup sugar (or a little more)
2 tablespoons apricot jam, apple jelly or
    marmalade

Roll out the pâte brisée dough thinly and use to line a 12 inch loose-bottomed, fluted flan pan. Prick all over and bake blind for 10 minutes.

Meanwhile, set aside 2 or 3 large apples; peel, core and chop the remainder. Cook the chopped apples with just enough water to stop them burning, until quite soft. Add the butter and sugar to taste (the mixture should still be quite tart) and beat to a smooth purée.

Peel, quarter and core the remaining apples and slice into transparently thin half moons.

Spread the apple purée in the pastry shell and cover with the apple slices arranged in circles and tightly overlapping. Sprinkle with a little more sugar and bake in the oven until the edges of the apple slices are just darkened.

When the tart has cooled, melt the jam, jelly or marmalade, strain it and brush over the apple slices to glaze the tart.

Bourdelots Normands *Baked Apples in Pastry Cases*

NORMANDY

A simple dessert, this is always popular with adults and children alike, and is sometimes known as "apples in their dressing gowns".

Preparation time: 15 minutes (plus pastry)
Cooking time: 40 to 45 minutes
Oven temperature: 425°; reduced to 375°
To serve: 4

1 cup confectioners' sugar
$\frac{1}{4}$ cup butter
4 large apples, peeled and cored
$\frac{1}{2}$ quantity pâte feuilletée (see page 115) or
  puff pastry
1 egg yolk
1 tablespoon water
light cream for serving

Work all but 1 tablespoon of the sugar into the butter. Stuff the center of each apple with this mixture.

Roll out the pâte feuilletée dough and cut into four large squares. Place an apple in the center of each square, bring up the corners to make a neat package and seal the edges. Decorate with any scraps of leftover dough. Place on a buttered baking sheet.

Mix the egg yolk with the water and brush the outside of each package. Bake in the preheated oven for 15 minutes, then reduce the temperature and bake for a further 25 to 30 minutes.

Sprinkle with the remaining sugar and serve warm, with cream.

Beignets De Fruits A La Lilloise *Fruit Fritters*

FLANDERS

Like most of the dishes of this region, this is a warming and sustaining dessert, but the batter is exceptionally light and delicious. You can use any number of differing fruits to add variety. Take care not to eat the fritters too quickly, as the fruits retain heat longer than the batter and it is easy to burn your tongue!

Preparation time: 30 minutes (plus 1 hour resting)
Cooking time: 20 to 30 minutes
To serve: 6 to 8

2 cups flour
pinch of salt
2 eggs
1$\frac{1}{2}$ cups beer
1 tablespoon vegetable oil
2 large apples, peeled, cored and sliced or
  cut into rings
2 bananas, cut into chunks
2 oranges, peeled and segmented
6 tablespoons sugar
1 tablespoon brandy
2 egg whites
oil for deep frying

Sift the flour and salt into a bowl and make a well in the center. Beat the 2 eggs with all but 2 tablespoons of the beer, pour into the center of the bowl and work into a smooth batter. Add the oil and leave to rest for 1 hour.

Arrange the fruit on separate plates, sprinkle with $\frac{1}{4}$ cup of the sugar and dribble on the remaining beer and the brandy. Leave to marinate while the batter is resting.

Beat the egg whites until stiff and fold into the batter.

Heat oil in a deep-fat fryer to 300°.

Drain the fruit. Dip first the banana chunks into the batter, drop into the hot oil and fry for 4 minutes, turning them over halfway through. Do the same with the apples and oranges, but give the apple fritters 6 minutes cooking time. Drain on paper towels and keep hot.

Sprinkle with the remaining sugar before serving.

Profiteroles Au Chocolat *Chocolate Cream Puffs*

ILE DE FRANCE

Choux pastry is a product of the sheer genius of French cooking, and these airy puffs, filled with a delicate crème chantilly and lightly enrobed with bitter chocolate sauce, must be about the most perfect dessert – light but rich, sweet without being cloying.

Preparation time: 30 minutes
Cooking time: 25 minutes for the puffs, 5 minutes for the sauce
Oven temperature: 425°
To serve: 6

Choux paste
1½ cups water
½ cup butter, preferably unsalted
pinch of salt
1 teaspoon sugar
1 cup sifted flour
4 eggs
1¼ cups crème chantilly (see page 121)

Sauce
¾ cup water
1 tablespoon cocoa powder
7 oz semisweet or bitter chocolate, broken into pieces
1 tablespoon butter

To make the choux paste put the water into a large saucepan, add the butter roughly cut into pieces, the salt and the sugar and bring slowly to a boil, stirring until the butter has melted. As soon as the water has come to a boil, take the saucepan off the heat and tip in all the flour. Beat with a wooden spoon until smooth, then return to a moderate heat and continue to beat until the mixture forms a ball and leaves the sides of the pan clean. Remove the pan from the heat again and beat in the eggs one by one, adding each only when the previous one has been completely absorbed.

Fill a pastry bag fitted with a plain tube with the choux paste and pipe small mounds onto a greased baking sheet, or drop small mounds onto the baking sheet with a teaspoon, making them as smooth as possible.

Bake in the oven until the puffs are well risen and pale brown. Remove the puffs from the oven and turn it off. Make an incision with the tip of a sharp knife in the side of each puff to let out the damp air. Lay each puff on its side on the baking sheet and return to the oven, leaving the oven door open. Dry for about 10 minutes, then cool on a wire rack.

When the puffs are quite cold and not too long before you are ready to serve them, fill each one with crème chantilly, and pile them in a serving dish.

Make the sauce by bringing the water and cocoa to a boil in a saucepan, stirring until smooth. Boil for 1 minute. Remove from the heat, add the chocolate and stir until the chocolate has melted. Add the butter cut into small pieces to give the sauce a glaze, and stir until smooth.

Pour the hot sauce over the profiteroles and serve.
Note: The profiteroles can also be filled with vanilla ice cream, giving the added pleasure of the contrast of temperatures.

Tarte Tatin *Caramelized Apple Tart*

ORLEANNAIS

The Demoiselles Tatin who lived in the Sologne area are credited with this famous upside-down apple tart, which is delicious and really not difficult to make. Use tart eating apples, such as the French Reinettes or American McIntosh.

Preparation time: 20 minutes (plus pastry)
Cooking time: 35 to 40 minutes
Oven temperature: 400°
To serve: 4

¼ cup butter
½ cup sugar
1 lb apples, peeled, cored and thickly sliced
½ quantity pâte brisée sucrée (see page 114)

Butter an 8 inch tart or quiche pan thickly, using half the butter. Sprinkle with half the sugar. Arrange the apple slices closely in circles in the pan.

Place the pan over a fairly high, even heat (electricity or solid fuel are more suitable than gas for this operation) and heat for 5 minutes to allow the butter and sugar to melt and lightly caramelize. Remove from the heat, dot the apples with the remaining butter and sprinkle with the remaining sugar.

Roll out the dough to the size of the pan. Cover the apples with the dough, allowing the edges to fall just inside the pan. Make several incisions in the dough lid with the point of a sharp knife to allow steam to escape.

Bake in the oven until the pastry is golden brown. Allow to cool a little before carefully unmolding the tart by inverting it onto a large dish. Serve warm or cold.

Savarin Montmorency

Savarin with Cherries
ILE DE FRANCE

A savarin is one of the classics of French pâtisserie, a light yeast dough baked in a tube pan and impregnated to saturation point with an alcoholic syrup. It is not difficult to make, provided you give yourself the time to go through all the processes in an unhurried way. It can also be made well ahead, kept frozen, and warmed through in a gentle oven. The classic savarin is made with a rum- or kirsch-flavored syrup and then decorated with blanched almonds and glacé cherries, and served with crème chantilly.

This particular version takes its name from the slightly tart cherries of Montmorency, a richly fertile orchard area outside Paris.

Preparation time: 2 hours minimum
Cooking time: 40 minutes
Oven temperature: 375°
To serve: 6 to 8

Savarin
1 cake (0.6 oz) compressed yeast
2 tablespoons sugar
2 cups flour
¾ cup lukewarm milk
pinch of salt
4 eggs
½ cup butter, melted

Filling
1 lb tart cherries, pitted (or use canned Morello cherries)
sugar to taste
large squeeze of lemon juice
¼ cup kirsch
1¼ cups crème chantilly (see page 121)

Savarin Montmorency

Cream the yeast with 1 teaspoon of the sugar and 1 teaspoon of the flour and stir in the milk. Leave in a warm place until frothy.

Sift the remaining flour and the salt into a large warmed bowl and make a well in the center. Pour in the yeast mixture and gradually work in the flour. Beat with a wooden spoon or knead with a lightly floured hand until the dough becomes elastic and leaves the side of the bowl clean. Cover with a clean cloth and leave in a warm place to rise to twice its original volume.

Beat the eggs lightly together with the remaining sugar and add the melted butter. Slowly beat this mixture into the dough and continue to beat with a wooden spoon until the dough becomes smooth and glossy. Turn into a buttered 10 inch savarin mold or tube pan and cover once more with a clean cloth. Leave to rise again in a warm place until the mixture comes to the top of the mold.

Bake in the oven until the top of the savarin is lightly browned and firm to the touch, and it has shrunk away a little from the sides of the mold. Turn out onto a wire cake rack and leave to cool.

Meanwhile, put the cherries in a saucepan and add enough water to come halfway up the cherries. Simmer until soft. Add sugar to taste and a squeeze of lemon juice. Drain the cherries, reserving the syrup. Add 3 tablespoons of the kirsch to the syrup.

If you are using canned cherries, drain them and add the lemon juice and kirsch to the syrup.

While the savarin is still slightly warm, place the cake rack over a dish and gently spoon over the lightly warmed cherry syrup until the savarin is completely impregnated, soft and spongy; it must not lose its shape.

Transfer carefully to a serving dish and pour over any syrup that has been caught in the dish under the rack. Sprinkle with the remaining kirsch. Pile the cherries into the center and top with a little of the crème chantilly. Serve the remaining crème chantilly separately.

Croissants

Sweet Pastry Crescents
ILE DE FRANCE

It is improbable that any French housewife would dream of baking her own croissants – after all, that is what the *boulanger* is there for. But for those with fond memories of breakfast and croissants in a Paris café, and no nearby source for croissants, they are well worth making at home. They are not difficult to make, but unless you want to stay up all night, they must be made at least a day ahead and either briefly reheated before serving or kept in the refrigerator overnight, and baked before breakfast in the morning. They also freeze well.

Preparation time: 1 day
Cooking time: 15 to 20 minutes
Oven temperature: 450°
Makes: 10 to 12 large croissants

1 cake (0.6 oz) compressed yeast
2 tablespoons lukewarm water
2 tablespoons sugar
2¼ cups bread flour
1 teaspoon salt
¾ cup lukewarm milk
1 tablespoon corn oil
½ cup butter
1 egg yolk
2 tablespoons cold milk

Dissolve the yeast in the warm water with 1 teaspoon of the sugar. Leave in a warm place until frothy.

Sift 2 cups of the flour into a large warm bowl with the salt, make a well in the center and pour in the yeast mixture. Add the warm milk with the remaining sugar dissolved in it, and the oil. Gently mix the flour into the liquid, then turn out onto a board lightly sprinkled with some of the remaining flour and knead very lightly, just until the dough begins to keep its shape. Use a rubber spatula if the dough is too soft to knead by hand and use as much of the rest of the flour on the board as necessary. Return the dough to the clean mixing bowl, cover with a clean cloth and leave in a fairly warm place for 3 to 4 hours or until it has risen to about three times its original volume.

Punch down the dough and leave to rise again for 1 to 2 hours, or until it has doubled in bulk.

When the dough is ready, flatten the butter between sheets of wax paper by beating it gently with a rolling pin.

Punch down the dough in the bowl, then place it on a lightly floured board and gently roll it into a rectangle three times as long as it is wide. Spread the butter over the two-thirds of the rectangle furthest away from you, leaving a ½ inch margin. Fold the unbuttered third towards the center, and then fold over again. Seal the edges.

Give the dough a half turn and roll out again into a rectangle. Fold into three once more, wrap loosely in a lightly floured plastic bag and leave in the refrigerator for 1 hour.

Take out of the refrigerator, deflate and leave for a few minutes at room temperature, then roll out into a rectangle and fold into three again. Replace in the refrigerator for at least another hour.

When the dough is ready, divide it in half and roll out the first half on a lightly floured board into a rectangle just under ¼ inch thick and about 6 inches wide. Cut the dough into squares, and each square into a triangle. Take the wide edge of one triangle and roll it over towards the point. Stretch the point a little to lengthen it, so that it can wrap right around the roll. Place on a lightly greased baking sheet with the point tucked underneath and bring the two ends slightly around towards each other to form a crescent shape. Repeat with the remaining dough.

Leave the prepared croissants in a warm place until they have risen to twice their size and feel springy to the touch. Mix the egg yolk with the milk and brush this glaze over the croissants. Bake in the oven for 15 to 20 minutes.

The prepared uncooked croissants may also be left in the refrigerator overnight. Leave at room temperature for 30 minutes before baking.

Croissants

Linzertorte *Spiced Raspberry Cake*

ALSACE

Although Linzertorte is really an Austrian specialty, it is also eaten in this part of France, where raspberries grow in ripe profusion. The Germanic influence on the cooking, seen here in the use of the cinnamon-spiced pastry, is very strong.

Preparation time: 30 minutes (plus 1 hour resting)
Cooking time: 35 to 40 minutes
Oven temperature: 350°
To serve: 6 to 8

$\frac{1}{2}$ cup butter
$\frac{1}{2}$ cup + 1 tablespoon sugar
1 small egg
finely grated rind of $\frac{1}{2}$ lemon
$1\frac{3}{4}$ cups flour
1 teaspoon ground cinnamon
$\frac{1}{2}$ teaspoon ground cloves
pinch of salt
1 cup ground almonds
1 pint raspberries

Cream the butter and $\frac{1}{2}$ cup of the sugar together and beat in the egg and the lemon rind. Sift the flour, cinnamon, cloves and salt into a bowl, then add gradually to the creamed mixture with the ground almonds. Gather the dough into a ball, cover and chill for 1 hour.

Roll out about two-thirds of the dough about $\frac{1}{4}$ inch thick and use to line a 9 inch flan or quiche pan, preferably a loose bottomed pan placed on a baking sheet. Spoon on the raspberries and sprinkle with the remaining sugar. Roll out the remaining dough and cut into strips $\frac{1}{2}$ inch wide. Make a lattice pattern over the tart. Seal the ends of the dough strips well to the edge of the tart.

Bake until the pastry is pale brown. Serve warm or cold.

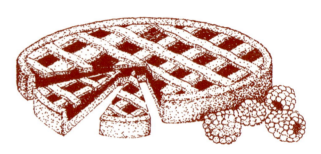

Kugelhopf *Yeast Cake*

ALSACE

Kugelhopf, Gugelhopf, Kougelhof, or Kugelhupf – whichever way you spell it, this light fruit cake or bread is one of the glories of Alsatian cooking. To look authentic, it should be baked in the slantingly fluted Kugelhopf mold, and should rise well above the mold during cooking.

Preparation time: 30 minutes (plus up to 2 hours rising)
Cooking time: 45 minutes
Oven temperature: 350°
To serve: 6 to 8

$\frac{1}{3}$ cup raisins
1 tablespoon kirsch or warm water
1 cake (0.6 oz) compressed yeast
$2\frac{1}{2}$ cups flour, sifted
$\frac{1}{4}$ cup sugar
5 tablespoons lukewarm milk
pinch of salt
2 eggs, beaten
$\frac{1}{2}$ cup butter, melted and cooled
$\frac{1}{2}$ cup almonds, cut into slivers
1 tablespoon confectioners' sugar

Soak the raisins in the kirsch or warm water.

Cream the yeast with 1 teaspoon of the flour and of the sugar. Add the warm milk. Cover and leave in a warm place until frothy.

Sift the remaining flour, salt and sugar into a bowl. Make a well in the center and pour in the frothy yeast mixture. Add the eggs and the melted butter. Begin to work in the flour with a wooden spoon, then turn out and knead on a lightly floured surface until the dough becomes elastic and comes away from the surface.

Put back into the lightly floured bowl, sprinkle with a little flour, cover with a clean cloth and leave to rise in a warm place for at least 1 hour, or until it has doubled in bulk.

Punch down and form into a fat sausage shape. Sprinkle on half the drained raisins and the almonds. Fold over and add the remaining raisins and almonds. Fold over once more and fit into the well-buttered kugelhopf mold (the mixture should not come more than halfway up). Leave to rise again until the mixture has doubled once more and risen to the top of the mold.

Bake for about 45 minutes. The top should have risen well above the top of the mold and should be light and springy to the touch. If the top appears to be browning too quickly, cover with a piece of buttered foil.

Allow the cake to cool for a few minutes, then turn out onto a wire cake rack and dredge liberally with confectioners' sugar.

Baba Au Rhum *Rum Baba*

ALSACE

LORRAINE

Legend has it that Stanilaus Leczinski, deposed King of Poland – later to become the father-in-law of Louis XV, and to whom Nancy owes its elegant Place Stanislas – introduced the baba to France. The Arabian Nights were the source of his inspiration.

Preparation time: 2 hours
Cooking time: 20 minutes
Oven temperature: 425°
To serve: 6 to 8

1 cake (0.6 oz) compressed yeast
2 tablespoons sugar
¾ cup lukewarm milk
2 cups flour
pinch of salt
4 eggs
½ cup butter, melted and cooled

Syrup
¾ cup sugar
2 cups water
2 strips of lemon rind
¼ cup rum
To decorate:
¾ cup crème chantilly (see page 121) or
    lightly whipped cream
glacé cherries

Cream the yeast with half the sugar and stir in the milk. Leave for 5 minutes in a warm place until frothy.

Sift the flour and salt into a warmed bowl and make a well in the center. Pour the yeast mixture into the center of the flour, and using a wooden spoon gradually work the flour into the liquid. Knead or beat with a wooden spoon for 5 minutes, until the dough becomes elastic and leaves the sides of the bowl clean. Cover with a damp cloth. Leave in a warm place until the dough has risen to twice its original volume.

Butter some baba pans or small tube pans.

Beat the eggs with the remaining sugar and pour in the butter. Beat this mixture slowly into the dough and continue to beat until the dough becomes smooth and glossy. Half fill each pan and leave to rise again in a warm place or until the dough has risen to the tops of the pans. Place in the oven and bake until the tops of the babas are lightly browned and quite firm to the touch, and they have shrunk slightly from the sides of their pans. Leave to cool a little, then turn out of the pans and leave to cool on a wire rack.

Meanwhile dissolve the sugar in the water in a saucepan, add the lemon rind and bring to a boil. Boil for 5 minutes. Leave to cool, then remove the strips of lemon rind from the syrup and add 3 tablespoons of the rum.

When the babas are still just warm, place them on a large dish and gently spoon the syrup over each one. The babas should be allowed to absorb as much syrup as they can without losing their shape. Leave to cool.

Just before serving sprinkle a little of the remaining rum over each one. Top each baba with a swirl of crème chantilly or whipped cream and crown with a cherry.

Tarte Alsacienne Au Rhubarbe *Alsatian Rhubarb Tart*

ALSACE

The creamy filling counteracts the sharpness of the rhubarb in this lovely mellow tart, which may be served as a dessert or with coffee, but will need to be eaten with pastry forks.

Preparation time: 30 minutes (plus pastry)
Cooking time: 50 minutes
Oven temperature: 375°
To serve: 6

1½ lb rhubarb, trimmed and cut into 1 inch
    lengths
¾ cup sugar
1 quantity pâte brisée sucrée (see page 114)
3 eggs, separated
¼ cup crème fraîche (see page 118) or
    heavy cream
finely grated rind of ½ lemon

Sprinkle the prepared rhubarb with half the sugar and leave for about 30 minutes to draw out the juice.

Meanwhile roll out the pastry and use to line a buttered 10 inch flan or quiche pan. Prick it well all over and bake blind for 10 minutes.

Drain the rhubarb, reserving the juice, and arrange it in a single layer in the pastry shell. Sprinkle with half the remaining sugar and return to the oven. Bake for 20 minutes, or until the rhubarb begins to soften.

Beat the egg yolks with the remaining sugar and beat in the rhubarb juice and the cream. Add the lemon rind. Beat the egg whites until stiff but not dry. Fold into the egg yolk mixture and pour this over the rhubarb.

Return the tart to the oven and bake for a further 20 minutes, or until the filling has set. Serve warm, or cold.

Les Macarons *Macaroons*

BEARN

Macaroons should be light, crisp on the outside and soft and moist inside. They should not be too sweet, and in the south of France a few bitter almonds or cracked peach or apricot kernels are often added to the almonds to give a slightly bitter tang. A similar effect can be achieved by using some unblanched almonds.

Preparation time: 10 minutes
Cooking time: 15 to 20 minutes
Oven temperature: 375°
To serve: 8 or more

2 cups finely ground almonds (see above)
2 cups sugar
½ teaspoon ground rice or cornstarch
4 egg whites
rice paper
split blanched almonds or halved glacé
    cherries to decorate (optional)

Mix together the almonds, sugar and ground rice or cornstarch in a bowl. Add the egg whites and combine thoroughly with a wooden spoon. Leave for a few minutes, then beat again briefly. Spread sheets of rice paper on baking sheets, rough side down. Using a teaspoon, make little mounds of the almond mixture on the sheets, leaving plenty of space between each one, to allow room for the macaroons to spread.

Press a split almond or half a glacé cherry in the center of each one, if you like. Bake in the oven for 15 to 20 minutes. Do not overcook, as the macaroons should be light and dry on the outside, but slightly tacky in the center.

Remove from the oven, break off each macaroon from the sheets of paper and leave to cool on a wire rack. Crumble off any surplus rice paper around the edges before serving.

Dacquoise *Hazelnut Meringue Layer Cake*

BEARN

Like most self-respecting French towns, the spa town of Dax, near the Spanish border, has its own specialty. This light and delectable cake is quite simple to make, but can be decorated to look very impressive.

Preparation time: 1 hour
Cooking time: 1 hour for the meringue and
   20 minutes for the butter cream
Oven temperature: 275°
To serve: 6 to 8

*Dacquoise, parfait Marie Brizard,
les macarons and
St Emilion au chocolat (page 141)*

Meringue Base
6 egg whites
pinch of salt
¼ teaspoon cream of tartar
¾ cup sugar
1 tablespoon cornstarch
¾ cup ground almonds
¾ cup ground hazelnuts

Butter Cream
4 egg yolks
½ cup sugar
1¼ cups milk
¾ cup unsalted butter
3 tablespoons kirsch, rum or very strong
   black coffee
2 oz semisweet or bitter chocolate, melted
   and cooled
1 cup powdered praline (see Croquante,
   page 127)

To decorate
½ cup toasted sliced almonds

Beat the egg whites with the salt until they begin to get foamy, then beat in the cream of tartar. Continue beating until the whites begin to stand in peaks, then start adding the sugar a spoonful at a time and continue until all the sugar has been absorbed and the meringue is smooth and bulky. Sift the cornstarch and the ground nuts together and gradually fold into the meringue using a spatula or metal spoon, and being careful not to let the meringue mixture lose air.

Butter and lightly flour two baking sheets, or line them with rice paper, and spoon on the meringue mixture, spreading and smoothing it to make two equal 10 to 12 inch diameter rounds. Place in the oven and bake for 1 hour, changing the meringue rounds around halfway through cooking until just firm to the touch and very slightly browned.

Leave to cool a little on a wire rack, then remove from the baking sheets or rice papers.

Make the butter cream by beating the egg yolks together with the sugar until pale. Bring the milk just to a boil, then pour onto the egg mixture in a thin stream, still beating. Pour into a clean pan and stir over a very gentle heat until the custard begins to thicken. Do not allow to boil. Pour back into the mixing bowl and allow to cool a little.

Cut the butter into small pieces and add them to the custard one by one, beating all the time, until all the butter has been absorbed. Beat in the kirsch, rum or coffee.

Pour half the mixture into another bowl, add the melted chocolate and beat until smooth. Add the powdered praline to the other half. Leave to cool.

When the two butter creams are quite cooled, sandwich the two meringue rounds together with the praline cream and decorate the top with the chocolate cream and flaked almonds.

Gâteau De Savoie *Sponge Cake*

SAVOIE

This is an excellent, simple sponge cake which can be eaten alone, or served to accompany fruit or ices. It may also be sandwiched together with some crème chantilly (see page 121) and soft fruit.

Preparation time: 20 minutes
Cooking time: 40 to 45 minutes
Oven temperature: 375°
To serve: 6 to 8

6 large eggs, separated
1 cup sugar
1 tablespoon orange flower water or water
¾ cup flour
¾ cup cornstarch or potato flour
pinch of salt

Beat the egg yolks with the sugar and orange flower water or water until light, pale and bulky. Sift the flour together with the cornstarch or potato flour and salt and carefully fold into the egg yolk mixture.

Whisk the whites until they stand in peaks, then fold into the cake batter. Divide between two greased and floured layer cake pans and bake until the cakes are just firm to the touch and have slightly shrunk away from the sides of the pans. Turn out and leave to cool before serving or putting together with cream.

Gâteaux A Noix *Walnut and Chocolate Slices*

AUVERGNE

The Auvergne is a walnut-growing area, and every *pâtisserie* has its own walnut specialty, such as these rich but light cream and chocolate-covered slices.

Preparation time: 40 minutes (plus pastry and chilling)
Cooking time: 40 to 45 minutes
Oven temperature: 375°
To serve: 6 to 8

½ quantity pâte brisée sucrée (see page 114)
3 eggs
2 tablespoons hot strong black coffee (made with instant coffee)
1 cup dark brown sugar
¼ cup unsalted butter, melted and cooled
¾ cup flour, sifted
1 cup fairly finely chopped walnuts

Topping
5 tablespoons unsalted butter
1½ cups confectioners' sugar
2 tablespoons strong black coffee
5 oz semisweet chocolate
1 tablespoon cream

Roll out the dough and use to line an 8 × 12 inch cake pan. Bake blind for 15 minutes.

Meanwhile beat the eggs with the hot coffee and sugar until thick and fluffy. Gently fold in the butter and flour and then the walnuts. Pour this mixture into the pastry shell and spread evenly. Return to the oven and bake for 25 to 30 minutes or until set. Leave to cool.

To make the topping, beat ¼ cup of the butter with the confectioners' sugar and coffee until smooth. Spread thinly over the cooled cake and chill to help the buttercream to set.

Break the chocolate into the top of a double boiler. Add the cream and set over simmering water. Stir until melted and smooth, then add the remaining butter cut into small pieces. Leave to cool, then spread evenly over the buttercream on the cake and leave to set. Cut the cake into squares before serving.

Poirat De Berry _Peppered Pear Tart_

BERRY

A piquant specialty of Berry, this is known locally as _piquenchagne_. The pepper just lifts the flavor in an unexpectedly pleasant way.

Preparation time: 30 minutes (plus 1 hour marinating)
Cooking time: 30 to 35 minutes
Oven temperature: 375°
To serve: 4 to 6

1 lb pears, peeled and cut into eighths
1 tablespoon brandy
2 tablespoons sugar
just under ½ quantity pâte brisée sucrée (see page 114)
finely ground black pepper
¾ cup crème fraîche (see page 118) or heavy cream

Sprinkle the pears with the brandy and 1 tablespoon of the sugar and leave for about 1 hour.

Roll out the dough and use to line an 8 inch flan or quiche pan. Prick the base and bake blind for 10 minutes.

Drain the pears, reserving the brandy, and lay them evenly in the pastry shell. Sprinkle with the remaining sugar, then lightly with pepper and bake until the pastry is cooked and the pears are tender.

Mix the brandy in which the pears have soaked with the cream. When the pears are cooked, pour the brandy mixture over the tart and return to the oven for another 5 minutes cooking to set.

Serve warm or cold.

St Emilion Au Chocolat _Chocolate Macaroon Dessert_

GUYENNE

The town of St. Emilion, near Bordeaux, is not only a great center for wine-growing, but has also lent its name to this rich chocolate dessert made with macaroons, which are one of the town's specialties.

Preparation time: 30 minutes plus chilling overnight
To serve: 8 to 10

½ cup unsalted butter
½ cup sugar
¾ cup milk
1 egg yolk
7 oz bitter or semisweet chocolate
1 batch macaroons (see page 138)
3 tablespoons brandy or Armagnac
Decoration (optional):
¾ cup whipped cream
chocolate shavings

Cream the butter and sugar together until very light and fluffy. Bring the milk almost to a boil, then mix a little of it into the egg yolk, to form a smooth cream. Break up the chocolate and add to the milk remaining in the saucepan. Return to a low heat and stir until the chocolate has completely melted and the mixture is absolutely smooth. Add the egg and stir until smooth. Slowly beat this chocolate cream into the butter and sugar mixture, and beat until the mixture is very light and smooth.

Arrange a layer of macaroons in the bottom of a glass or soufflé dish. Sprinkle with a little brandy or Armagnac. Smooth on a layer of the chocolate cream. Repeat until everything has been used up, ending with macaroons. Leave in the refrigerator overnight to mature. Decorate, if you like, with a layer of whipped cream, sprinkled with chocolate shavings, before serving.

Pavé Aux Marrons *Chocolate Chestnut Cake*

GUYENNE

This is a very rich cake, which can be eaten as a dessert or as a confection. The mixture can also be shaped into a yule log, decorated with a fork to give the appearance of bark, sprinkled with a little confectioners' sugar to look like snow, and decorated with hazelnuts for knots in the bark.

Preparation time: 15 minutes (plus peeling chestnuts)
Cooking time: 20 minutes
To serve: 6

1½ lb chestnuts, peeled
½ cup sugar
4 oz semisweet or bitter chocolate
½ cup unsalted butter

Frosting
4 oz semisweet or bitter chocolate
1 tablespoon water
1 tablespoon butter

Put the chestnuts into a large heavy saucepan, cover with cold water and bring to a boil. Simmer for about 20 minutes, or until they are tender. Drain and purée in a blender or food processor. Fold the sugar into the purée and leave to cool.

Melt the chocolate in a double boiler. Remove from the heat and stir until smooth, then add the butter, cut into small pieces, and stir until well combined. Work this into the chestnut mixture until you have a soft, smooth mixture.

Turn into a greased and lined cake pan and chill overnight. Frost with the chocolate melted with the water and butter, and cut into squares when set.

Or chill the mixture, then form into a yule log and leave overnight to set. Streak with the melted chocolate frosting and decorate as suggested above.

Serve with brandy-flavored crème chantilly (see page 121) if liked.

Clafoutis Aux Cerises *Baked Cherry Pudding*

LIMOUSIN

Clafoutis, a baked batter pudding with fruit, are eaten throughout France. This recipe comes from the Limousin, where some of the best cherries grow. Ripe but firm black cherries should be used.

Preparation time: 25 minutes (plus 1 hour marinating)
Cooking time: 40 to 45 minutes
Oven temperature: 425°
To serve: 6

1 lb black cherries, pitted
2 tablespoons kirsch or brandy
3 eggs
¼ cup granulated sugar
¾ cup flour, sifted
pinch of salt
1½ cups milk
¼ cup butter
confectioners' sugar

Leave the cherries to soak in the kirsch or brandy for at least 1 hour.

Beat the eggs together with the sugar, then mix in the flour and salt, followed by the milk and half the butter, melted.

Butter a shallow baking dish or cake pan very generously and pour in a thin layer of the batter. Bake for 5 minutes or until just set.

Drain the cherries and distribute them evenly over the batter. Pour the cherry liquid into the remaining batter, beat again and pour over the cherries. Dot with the remaining butter.

Return to the oven and bake until the top is set and lightly browned. Sprinkle generously with confectioners' sugar and serve warm.

Index

143